After Worldview

After Worldview

Christian Higher Education in Postmodern Worlds

Edited by J. Matthew Bonzo and Michael Stevens

Dordt College Press

Cover design by Todd Montsma
Layout by Carla Goslinga

Printed in the United States of America.

Dordt College Press   www.dordt.edu/dordt_press
498 Fourth Avenue NE
Sioux Center, Iowa 51250
United States of America

ISBN: 978-0-932914-74-3

Library of Congress Cataloging-in-Publication Data

After worldview: Christian higher education in postmodern worlds/ edited by J. Matthew Bonzo and Michael Stevens.
    p. cm.
  ISBN 978-0-932914-74-3 (pbk. : alk. paper)
1.   Christianity—Philosophy—Congresses. I. Bonzo, J. Matthew,
II.   Stevens, Michael Roger.
    BR100.A38 2009
    230.01—dc22
        2008055977

Table of Contents

Part IV: Worldview in the Classroom

Introduction

The essays collected in this work were originally presented at the *After Worldview* conference, which took place on the campus of Cornerstone University on 16–18 September 2004. The conference brought together many of the leading voices on Christian worldview in North America to examine questions regarding the nature and role of worldview in a postmodern world.

The conference was organized by the Civitas Center of Cornerstone University. The Civitas Center, in its quest to educate wise citizens, has been carefully considering the role of worldview in providing a deeply rooted Christian education at the university level. In pursuing this task, a reading group composed of members of the faculty and administration read many of the important recent texts regarding Christian worldview. We included on our reading list David Naugle's important *Worldview: The History of a Concept*, Al Wolters' foundational *Creation Regained*, Jim Olthuis's formative essay "On Worldviews," the engaging works of Brian Walsh and Richard Middleton, and the widely influential books of Jim Sire.

As we read and discussed these significant works, we became aware of both an ambiguity with the term worldview and a growing dissatisfaction among some scholars with the use of worldview language. Our reading of critical evaluations of Christian worldview and an increased sensitivity to the changing context of higher education led us to the conclusion that the time was right to bring together as many of the significant thinkers on worldview as possible to help us reflect upon a broad set of concerns regarding the definition and functioning of Christian worldview. By naming the conference—and now this volume—*After Worldview*, we allowed for room in thinking about worldview. The "after" was not limited to meaning it was time to get past worldview, but could also indicate a search for conformity.

As these thinkers revisited the concept of worldview, each approached it from a slightly different angle. However, there are a couple of notable similarities emphasized in various essays. One confluence of the papers could be summarized as the call for a hospitable use of worldview. Many of the following essays are written from the neo-Kuyperian perspective.

These writers express a concern about the increasing tendency among some evangelicals to use worldview "tests" as a measure of orthodoxy. Furthermore, there is a resistance to developing worldview categories as a means to "pigeonhole" thinkers, especially non-Christian ones.

Another convergence of the essays is the emphasis placed on understanding worldview as what Wolters describes as "prescientific" or "pretheoretical" and Naugle calls "kardioptic." Sharing in this conception differentiates the contributors from other Christian thinkers who understand worldview as an intellectual or theoretical system. The difference in approach is important. For the neo-Kuyperian thinkers, commitment precedes theoretical investigation and articulation, whether it is philosophical or theological. The construction of Christian Worldview as a means of doing apologetics typically understands worldview as being built upon some shared rational framework. In these essays, the central issue is not one of rational justification, but the spirituality of worldview.

The papers contained in this volume, as well as the many papers given at the conference but not included here, give thoughtful and nuanced examination to important issues regarding a Christian understanding and use of worldview. If the conference was any indication, a vibrant discussion on these matters will continue for quite some time.

Acknowledgments

Many hands have cultivated this volume, so there are many thanks to share. For the preparatory work on the After Worldview Conference of September 2004, we thank our colleagues in the Civitas Center at Cornerstone University, especially Randall Burghart and the many student helpers, led by our indispensable assistant Miranda Gardner. We also want to express our gratitude to Steven Haskill, who helped with the organization of this book and spent many hours getting the text into publishable form.

For participating in our plenary sessions, we thank our speakers and respondents: David Naugle, Calvin Seerveld, James Sire, Jim Olthuis, Al Wolters, Richard Middleton, Jeffrey Davis, David Urban, Craig Mattson, Jim Herrick, and Doug Mohrmann. Our thanks also go out to all of those who gave papers in our concurrent sessions and indeed to all who attended the conference in any capacity, since the informal conversations seemed to burgeon throughout the weekend. We appreciate the support of Cornerstone's administrative leadership: President Rex Rogers, Executive Vice President Bob Nienhuis, Academic Vice President By Baylis, and Dean of General Studies Tim Detwiler—with a special thanks to the Director of Food Services, Cindy Wiltheiss.

As for the fruit of the conference in book form, we thank all of the participants who revisited their talks for publication in this volume, as well as Professor Roy Anker from Calvin College for entering into the conversation with his brief essay on film and antithesis. Of course, the whole project would have stalled without the willingness of John Kok at Dordt College Press to encourage us and to provide a publishing forum. This has been a time of rich, blessed conversation, and we hope the book will continue that process.

J. Matthew Bonzo and Michael Stevens
Grand Rapids, Michigan

Part I

A Historical Overview of Worldview

Worldview: History, Theology, Implications

David Naugle

In the introductory remarks to his book *Heretics*, G. K. Chesterton writes these crucial words about the importance of worldview:

> But there are some people, nevertheless—and I am one of them—who think that the most practical and important thing about a man is still his view of the universe. We think that for a landlady considering a lodger, it is important to know his income, but still more important to know his philosophy. We think that for a general about to fight an enemy, it is important to know the enemy's numbers, but still more important to know the enemy's philosophy. We think the question is not whether the theory of the cosmos affects matters, but whether, in the long run, anything else affects them.[1]

This quote was striking when I first read it, and it remains so still today. After all, what could be more important or powerful than the way individuals conceptualize reality? Is anything more fundamental than a person's set of presuppositions and assumptions about the basic makeup of the universe? What is more significant than a human being's foundational system of beliefs? Is there anything more profound or influential than the answers to the deeper questions that the very presence of the universe poses to us all? In agreement, then, with Gilbert Keith Chesterton, I submit that the most practical and important thing about a human being is his or her view of the universe and theory of the cosmos—that is, the content and implications of one's worldview.

For this reason, I believe that conceiving of biblical faith as a world-

---

1   G. K. Chesterton, *Heretics, in The Complete Works of G. K. Chesterton*, vol. 1, ed. David Dooley (San Francisco: Ignatius, 1986), 41.

view has been one of the more important developments in the recent history of the Church. Though such a generous vision of reality is rooted in the best of the Church's tradition, for various reasons—especially the reductionistic pressures stemming from modernism—this bigger biblical picture of things has virtually vanished. "We have rather lost sight of the idea," Dorothy Sayers once noted, "that Christianity is supposed to be an interpretation of the universe."[2] This larger perspective is too often hidden under a basket and its light almost extinguished.

In this contemporary setting of dwarfed versions of the faith, the concept of worldview has, in a sense, come to the rescue. It offers the Church a fresh perspective on the holistic nature, cosmic dimensions, and universal applications of the faith. Plus, the explanatory power, intellectual coherence, and pragmatic effectiveness of a Christian worldview not only make it exceedingly relevant for believers personally, but also establish it as a solid foundation for vigorous cultural and academic engagement. For these reasons, then, we will do well to understand as much as we can about the *history* of the concept of worldview, its *theological* meaning, and its *implications* on a variety of prominent human enterprises. That is what I seek to accomplish in this essay. We begin, then, with a look at the origin of worldview as a concept and its history in the evangelical Church.

A History of the Concept of Worldview

There is virtually universal recognition that the notable Prussian philosopher Immanuel Kant coined the term *Weltanschauung*, that is, "worldview," in his work *Critique of Judgment*, published in 1790. It originates in a quintessential Kantian paragraph that emphasizes the power of the perception of the human mind. Kant writes, "If the human mind is nonetheless to be able even to think the given infinite without contradiction, it must have within itself a power that is supersensible, whose idea of the noumenon cannot be intuited but can yet be regarded as the substrate underlying what is mere appearance, namely, our intuition of the world" (*Weltanschauung*).[3] That last phrase—"our intuition of the world"—is an English translation of Kant's coined German term *Weltanschauung*.

---

2   Dorothy L. Sayers, 1937–1944: *From Novelist to Playwright*, vol. 2, *The Letters of Dorothy Sayers*, ed. Barbara Reynolds, preface by P. D. James (New York: St. Martin's, 1998), 158.
3   Immanuel Kant, *Critique of Judgment: Including the First Introduction*, trans. and intro. Werner S. Pluhar, with a foreword by Mary J. Gregor (Indianapolis: Hackett, 1987), 111–12 (emphasis original).

The context of this quotation suggests that for Kant, *Weltanschauung* means something rather simple, like a perception of the world gained empirically. Martin Heidegger notes that Kant employed *Weltanschauung* in reference to the *mundus sensibilis*, that is, as a "world-intuition in the sense of contemplation of the world given to the senses."[4]

From its coinage in Kant, who used the term only once and for whom it was of minor significance, it evolved rather quickly to refer to an intellectual conception of the universe from the perspective of a human knower. Kant's Copernican revolution in philosophy, with its emphasis on the knowing and willing self as the cognitive and moral center of the universe, created the conceptual space in which the notion of worldview could flourish. The term was adopted by Kant's successors and soon became a celebrated concept in German intellectual life.

Weltanschauung captured the imaginations not only of the German intelligentsia, but also of thinkers throughout Europe and beyond. The term's success is seen by how readily it was adopted by writers in other European languages either as a loanword, especially in the Romance languages, or as a copy word in the idiom of Slavic and Germanic languages.

This concept, indeed, had legs. Given its prominence, it was impossible for it to remain isolated on the Continent for long. Soon it crossed the channel to Great Britain and made its way across the Atlantic to the United States. According to the *Oxford English Dictionary*, within seventy-eight years of its inaugural use in Kant's *Critique of Judgment*, *Weltanschauung* entered the English language in 1868 in its naturalized form as "worldview." Ten years later, the German term itself gained currency as a loan word in Anglo-American academic discourse. Since their midnineteenth-century beginnings, both *Weltanschauung* and worldview have flourished and become significant terms in the thought and vocabulary of thinking people in the English-speaking world.

Throughout the nineteenth century, therefore, *Weltanschauung* became enormously popular. By the 1890s, the Scottish theologian James Orr could say that as a concept, it had become "in a manner indispensable."[5] It is no wonder, then, that Orr himself, as well as Abraham Kuyper, capitalized on its notoriety as a convenient and potent expression to configure their respective versions of a comprehensive Christian worldview of Calvinist persuasion.

---

4   Martin Heidegger, *The Basic Problems of Phenomenology, in Studies in Phenomenology and Existential Philosophy*, trans., intro., and lexicon Albert Hofstadter (Bloomington: Indiana University, 1982), 4.
5   James Orr, *The Christian View of God and the World as Centering in the Incarnation* (New York: Scribner, 1887; reprint, *The Christian View of God and the World*, with a foreword by Vernon C. Grounds, Grand Rapids: Kregel Publications, 1989), 365.

Original Worldview Thinkers in Protestant Evangelicalism

The headwaters of the worldview tradition among Protestant evangelicals can be traced to two primary sources, both of which flow from the theological wellsprings of the Reformer from Geneva, John Calvin (1509–1564).[6] The first is the Scottish Presbyterian theologian, apologist, minister, and educator James Orr (1844–1913). The second is the Dutch neo-Calvinist theologian and statesman Abraham Kuyper (1837–1920). Appropriating the concept from the broader intellectual milieu on the European continent, these two seminal thinkers introduced the vocabulary of worldview into the current of Reformed Christian thought and from there into the broader evangelical church. In their creative efforts, they gave birth to an agenda to conceive of biblical faith as a vigorous, coherent vision of reality that opened up Christianity to full flower with benefits inside the Church and as a way to meet the challenges of the modern world head on.

James Orr. The opportunity for James Orr to articulate the Christian faith as a worldview arose when he was invited by the United Presbyterian Theological College in Edinburgh to present the first of the Kerr Lectures, whose stated purpose was for "the promotion of the study of Scientific theology."[7] These addresses took him three years to prepare, were delivered in 1891, and were published in 1893 as *The Christian View of God and the World as Centering in the Incarnation.*[8] In this book, he devoted the first chapter and several endnotes to the concept of worldview in general and to the idea of a Christian worldview in particular.

According to Orr, a worldview denoted "the widest view which the mind can take of things in the effort to grasp them together as a whole

---

6   Calvin apparently recognized that his own theological system constituted the basis for a Christian philosophy, which may be roughly analogous to a Christian worldview. In introducing the subject matter of his *Institutes of the Christian Religion*, he informs his readers that God provides guidance to help simple people discover "the sum of what God meant to teach them in his Word." He then says that this cannot be done in any better way than "to treat the chief and weightiest matters comprised in the Christian philosophy." See his *Institutes of the Christian Religion, The Library of Christian Classics*, vol. 20, ed. John T. McNeill, trans. and indexed Ford Lewis Battles (Philadelphia: Westminster, 1960), 6.

7   *Proceedings of the Synod of the United Presbyterian Church* (1887): 489–90, quoted in Scorgie, *The Call for Continuity: Continuity: The Theological Contribution of James Orr.* (Macon, Ga.: Mercer University, 1988), 47.

8   James Orr, *The Christian View of God and the World as Centering in the Incarnation* (Edinburgh: Andrew Eliot, 1893). This book has undergone many editions and reprints, the most recent being *The Christian View of God and the World*, foreword Vernon C. Grounds (Grand Rapids: Kregel Publications, 1989).

from the standpoint of some particular philosophy or theology."[9] The Christian faith in Orr's opinion provides such a standpoint, developing its loftiest principle and view of life into "an ordered whole."[10] While explaining and defending Christian doctrines atomistically may have its place, Orr believed that the worldview concept enabled him to set forth and validate Christianity in its entirety as a coherent system. Given the increasingly anti-Christian *Zeitgeist* of the late nineteenth century, he perceived "that if Christianity is to be effectually defended from the attacks made upon it, it is the comprehensive method which is rapidly becoming the more urgent."[11] Nothing less than a fresh, coherent presentation of the Christian definition of reality in all its fullness would be adequate for the times.

Orr's biblically based worldview was centered in the incarnation, as the second half his book title indicates. Belief in Jesus entailed a whole host of additional convictions, forming an overall view of things. He writes:

> He who with his whole heart believes in Jesus as the Son of God is thereby committed to much else besides. He is committed to a view of God, to a view of man, to a view of sin, to a view of Redemption, to a view of human destiny, found only in Christianity. This forms a *"Weltanschauung,"* or "Christian view of the world," which stands in marked contrast with theories wrought out from a purely philosophical or scientific standpoint.[12]

For Orr, then, biblical belief in Jesus Christ logically entailed a commitment to a complete *Weltanschauung*. Christianity was a Christocentric vision of life, a revolutionary and apologetically expedient approach to the faith necessitated by the challenges of modernity at its apex.

Both Gordon H. Clark and Carl F. H. Henry appear to be the heirs of Orr's worldview legacy. As a professional philosopher writing from an evangelical point of view, Gordon Clark (1902–1986) was recognized at the height of his powers as "perhaps the dean of those twentieth century American philosophers who have sought to develop a Christian *Weltanschauung* consistent with the Christian Scriptures."[13] Indeed, the title and content of one of his best-known books—*A Christian View of Men*

---

9   Orr, *The Christian View*, 3.
10   Orr, *The Christian View*, 3.
11   Orr, *The Christian View*, 4.
12   Orr, *The Christian View*, 4.
13   Ronald H. Nash, preface to *The Philosophy of Gordon H. Clark: A Festschrift*, ed. Ronald H. Nash (Philadelphia: Presbyterian and Reformed, 1968), 5.

and Things—suggests continuity with Orr's work.[14]

Orr's worldview tradition influenced the late Carl F. H. Henry (1913–2003) as well. During his student days at Wheaton College, Henry became enamored of comprehending and defending the faith as a total "world-life view" by reading Orr's volume. In his autobiography, he recalls, "It was James Orr's great work, *The Christian View of God and the World*, used as a Senior text in theism, that did the most to give me a cogently comprehensive view of reality and life in a Christian context."[15] Through Henry, the idea of worldview in general and the notion of the Christian worldview in particular have been promoted widely among professional theologians and the evangelical public. "His emphasis was always on the big picture," said Kenneth Kantzer. "Above all he sought to think clearly and effectively, consistently and comprehensively, about the total Christian world and life view."[16] This outlook animated his words in the influential manifesto *The Uneasy Conscience of American Fundamentalism* (1947) that challenged the born-again church to trace out and apply the redemptive power of the Christian gospel to the totality of human thought and culture.

Abraham Kuyper. Meanwhile, to backtrack just a bit, about the same time James Orr was publishing his influential worldview volume in Scotland, a similar agenda was developing on the European continent. This time it was being promoted by an increasingly prominent Dutch ecclesiastical and political figure named Abraham Kuyper. A noted journalist, politician, educator, and theologian with mosaic vigor, Kuyper is especially remembered as the founder of the Free University of Amsterdam in 1880 and as the Prime Minister of the Netherlands from 1901–1905. The source of this man's remarkable contributions is found in a powerful spiritual vision derived from the theology of the Protestant Reformers (primarily Calvin) that centered upon the sovereignty of the biblical God over all aspects of reality.

For Kuyper, if non-Christian worldviews characterized by idolatry and religious insubordination are worked out across the whole spectrum of life (which they are), then likewise Christianity must also be articulated in terms of a comprehensive vision of reality engendering the worship of

---

14 Gordon H. Clark, *A Christian View of Men and Things: An Introduction to Philosophy* (Grand Rapids: Eerdmans, 1951; reprint, Grand Rapids: Baker, 1981).

15 Carl F. H. Henry, *Confessions of a Theologian: An Autobiography* (Waco: Word, 1986), 75.

16 Kenneth S. Kantzer, "Carl Ferdinand Howard Henry: An Appreciation," in *God and Culture: Essays in Honor of Carl F. H. Henry*, ed. D. A. Carson and John D. Woodbridge (Grand Rapids: Eerdmans, 1993), 372.

God and submission to his will in all things.[17] Indeed, when Kuyper was at the height of his powers, he had the opportunity to demonstrate that his beloved Calvinism was more than a just a church polity or doctrinaire religion, but rather an all-encompassing *Weltanschauung* when he was invited to deliver the prestigious Stone Lectures at Princeton University in 1898. These addresses and the book that resulted from them, *Lectures on Calvinism*, became a second influential source for conceiving of Christianity as a worldview among evangelical Protestants.[18]

Interestingly enough, Kuyper's reading of James Orr's recently published *The Christian View of God and the World* was likely a turning point in his own thinking. It underscored the value of *Weltanschauung* in his eyes and prompted him to cast his entire lectures on Calvinism as a comprehensive vision of the world and of life within it. Indeed, the similarities between the two thinkers on worldview are remarkable, and it appears that Kuyper drew considerably from Orr's thought on the topic.[19]

Like Orr before him, Kuyper saw his present cultural moment defined in both Europe and America by a life-and-death struggle between two antithetical worldviews or, as he called them, "life-systems." As Orr proposed in his own lectures, Kuyper argued that a piecemeal apologetic approach must be replaced with a strategy that countered an all-encompassing modernism with a comprehensive Christian *Weltanschauung*. In his concluding lecture on "Calvinism and the Future," Kuyper makes this point with great clarity and power:

> With such a coherent world and life-view, firmly resting on its principle and self-consistent in its splendid structure, Modernism now confronts Christianity; and against this deadly danger, ye, Christians, cannot successfully defend your sanctuary, but by placing in opposition to all this, *a life and world-view of your own, founded as firmly on the base of your own principle, wrought out with the same clearness and glittering in an equally logical consistency.*[20]

In his lectures on Calvinism, therefore, Kuyper presents Reformed Christianity as a total framework of biblical thought; draws out its implications in the areas of religion, politics, science, and art; and suggests the kind of role it ought to play in the future of the world. So conceived and articulated, it could take its place alongside the other great systems of hu-

---

17 R. D. Henderson, "How Abraham Kuyper Became a Kuyperian," *Christian Scholars Review* 22 (1992): 22, 34–35.
18 Abraham Kuyper, *Lectures on Calvinism* (Grand Rapids: Eerdmans, 1994).
19 Peter S. Heslam, *Creating a Christian Worldview: Abraham Kuyper's Lectures on Calvinism* (Grand Rapids: Eerdmans, 1998), 93–94.
20 Kuyper, *Lectures on Calvinism*, 189–90 (emphasis original).

man thought, including paganism, Islamism, Romanism, and modernism, and be effective in the spiritual and intellectual warfare being waged in the modern world for cultural dominance.

This conception of Calvinistic Christianity subsumed under the rubric of worldview was appropriated by Kuyper's followers—the Dutch neo-Calvinists or Kuyperians—and passed down to subsequent generations.[21] Eventually it migrated with them across the Atlantic, and became a significant theme among them as an immigrant community in North America. Both Calvin College in Grand Rapids, Michigan, and the Institute for Christian Studies in Toronto, Ontario, Canada—where Kuyperian ideals and worldview thinking have flourished—were birthed out of this tradition.

Francis A. Schaeffer. This forceful Reformed interpretation of Christian faith also influenced Francis A. Schaeffer (1912–1984), without whom no discussion on the evangelical history of worldview would be complete. He affirmed what is now a commonplace that all people have a worldview and nobody, whether ditch digger or professional thinker, can live without one. Philosophy is the only unavoidable occupation.[22] Also, his rich interpretation of a Christianity that was intellectually credible and embraced the whole of life was uniquely attractive to many. Indeed, his discussion of a significant range of cultural issues from a Christian point of view was quite refreshing after decades of fundamentalist obscurantism.

This Swiss missionary and founder of L'Abri Fellowship recommended a Christian worldview as the only realistic answer to the pervasive emptiness and despair of modern secular life. Schaeffer was passionate for the comprehensive system of "true truth" set forth in the Scriptures. In *Escape from Reason*, Schaeffer says, "I love the biblical system as a system,"[23] and in *The God Who Is There*, he explains why:

> The Christian system (what is taught in the whole Bible) is a unity of thought. Christianity is not just a lot of bits and pieces—there is a beginning and an end, a whole system of truth, and this system is the only system that will stand up to all the questions that are presented to us as we face the reality of existence.[24]

---

21   For example, Herman Bavinck (1854–1921), D. H. T. Vollenhoven (1892–1978), Herman Dooyeweerd (1894–1977), Cornelius Van Til (1895–1987).

22   Francis A. Schaeffer, *He Is There and He Is Not Silent*, vol. 1, *The Complete Works of Francis A. Schaeffer: A Christian Worldview*, 2nd ed. (Wheaton: Crossway Books, 1982), 279–80.

23   Francis A. Schaeffer, *Escape from Reason*, vol. 1, *The Complete Works of Francis A. Schaeffer: A Christian Worldview*, 2nd ed. (Wheaton: Crossway Books, 1982), 221.

24   Francis A. Schaeffer, *The God Who Is There*, vol. 1, *The Complete Works of Francis A.*

Schaeffer articulated his understanding of the biblical *Weltanschauung* in the first three books he published. The trilogy of *The God Who Is There*, *Escape from Reason*, and *He Is There and He Is Not Silent* formed the hub of his system, and his other works gave expression to his conception of the Christian vision as though they were spokes.[25] An entire generation of evangelicals, myself included, cut their worldview teeth on Schaeffer's work and thus has him to thank for stimulating an abiding interest in cultivating a comprehensive, systematic understanding of biblical faith with all of its attendant personal, intellectual, and cultural implications.

Collectively, then, these noted thinkers handed the worldview baton off to others who have been running with it quite effectively ever since. Brian Walsh, Richard Middleton, Albert Wolters, Arthur Holmes, James Sire, Charles Colson, and Nancy Pearcey are just a few of the authors who have promoted worldview thinking and living vigorously in the evangelical community.[26] In fact, in the entire history of worldview, no single philosophic school or religious community has given more sustained attention to or taken more advantage of this concept than Protestant evangelicals. This extensive use of the worldview concept carries with it certain assets, to be sure. But its use, perhaps even its overuse, also fosters some liabilities as well. Some debate the suitability of the notion in the Church, and confusion exists regarding its basic definition and character. In light of these and other issues that have clouded the worldview sky, I think it prudent to offer some theological reflections on the worldview concept in an attempt to clarify its role and identity in the evangelical Christian community where God's Word reigns as the supreme authority.

Theological Reflections on Worldview

In tracing out the history of the worldview concept in a variety of disciplines, it is fascinating to observe how basic descriptions of it reflect the worldview of the one offering the description. For example, Hegel's idealism, Kierkegaard's theism, Dilthey's historicism, Nietzsche's athe-

Schaeffer: A Christian Worldview, 2nd ed. (Wheaton: Crossway Books, 1982), 178.

25   The subtitle to Schaeffer's *Complete Works* is aptly designated "A Christian Worldview." Volume one deals with a Christian view of philosophy containing the three books mentioned above. Volume two deals with a Christian view of the Bible as truth. Volume three deals with a Christian view of spirituality. Volume four deals with a Christian view of the church. Volume five deals with a Christian view of the West. See Francis A. Schaeffer, *The Complete Works of Francis A. Schaeffer: A Christian Worldview*, 2nd ed., 5 vols. (Wheaton: Crossway Books, 1982).

26   David K. Naugle, *Worldview: The History of a Concept* (Grand Rapids: Eerdmans, 2002), Appendix A.

ism, Husserl's phenomenology, Jaspers' existentialism, Heidegger's ontologism, Wittgenstein's linguisticism, and the postmodernists' skepticism affected their respective hypotheses on worldview deeply. There is a sociological relativity to theorizing about worldview. Any view of worldview, therefore, is itself worldview dependent.

The question, then, emerges regarding the implications of a Christian worldview on worldview theory: what nuances does Christian theism as a *Weltanschauung* impart to the notion of *Weltanschauung* itself? How do Scripture and theology contribute to our understanding of this important idea?

This is an important task. Several critics have voiced concerns about possible menacing connotations associated with worldview when it comes to its use in the Church. By the time James Orr and Abraham Kuyper appropriated worldview for Christian purposes, it had already become drenched with modern implications. Within the framework of European idealism and romanticism, it connoted a thoroughgoing subjectivism and a person- or culture-relative perspective on reality. Consequently, worldviews were considered not "facts" but "values" and were consigned to the domain of private life.

The status of worldview becomes even more questionable in the context of postmodernism, which is characterized famously by an "incredulity toward metanarratives."[27] As reified constructs and as instruments of power and violence, worldviews must be "deconstructed" and shown to be nothing more than privatized micronarratives possessing little, if any, public authority.[28]

Given this background, evangelicals who employ the language of worldview regularly would be irresponsible if they were to neglect the historical development of this term and the significations it has acquired in modern and postmodern parlance. The question, then, is this: Can worldview be regenerated and baptized in biblical waters, cleansing it of modern and postmodern impurities, making it useful for Christian service?[29] I believe that it can.

If believers can be sanctified and if culture can be renewed, then

---

27   Jean-François Lyotard, *The Postmodern Condition: A Report on Knowledge, Theory and History of Literature*, vol. 10, trans. Geoff Bennington and Brian Massumi, foreword Fredric Jameson (Minneapolis: University of Minnesota, 1984), xxiv.
28   William V. Rowe, "Society after the Subject, Philosophy after the Worldview." In Marshall, et al., *Stained Glass*, 156–83.
29   Sander Griffioen, Richard Mouw, and Paul Marshall, ed., "Introduction," in *Stained Glass: Worldviews and Social Science*, Christian Studies Today (Lanham: University Press of America, 1989), 8, 10.

perhaps an intellectual conception can be converted as well. Even biblical authors themselves frequently appropriated language and concepts from their surrounding cultures and used them in the context of Holy Scripture with fresh theistic meaning to convey the unique content and wisdom of divine revelation. Has this not provided something of a precedent that has been followed in postcanonical theological reflection when it comes to employing nonbiblical terms and concepts to convey biblical themes and truths? Perhaps worldview falls into this category!

As a matter of fact, plucking the concept of *Weltanschauung* out of recent intellectual discourse and using it for Christian purposes can be compared admirably to St. Augustine's ancient strategy of appropriating pagan notions and employing them suitably in the church. He believed firmly that all truth was God's truth, and in his famous "Egyptian Gold" analogy in *De Doctrina Christiana*, he explains on the basis of a story found in Exodus 11–12 how truth can be recovered and utilized in superior ways by believers. For just as the Israelites appropriated the gold and silver of the Egyptians and used it in service to God, so Christians can appropriate the intellectual gold and silver of non-Christian thinkers and employ it in Christian service as well.[30]

I submit that the notion of worldview is a valuable piece of "Egyptian gold." If we follow St. Augustine's reasoning, we can propose that believers need to claim it for their own and convert it to Christian use. In doing so, however, we must cleanse it of its pagan associations, reform it biblically, and make it a concept serviceable to the kingdom of God. As St. Paul says in 2 Corinthians 10:5b, ". . . we are taking every thought captive to the obedience of Christ." The theological reflections that follow will attempt to do just that.

My goal in reflecting on worldview theologically is to discern what inferences or connotations are built into this notion when it is examined from a Christian standpoint. Overall, I will make four assertions that impart biblically based nuances to worldview that stand in noticeable contrast to its secular significations.

Issues of objectivity. To the extent that the term *worldview* has been tinted or tainted for over two centuries with the hues of relativism, an affirmation of theological, cosmological, and moral objectivity rooted in God is the antidote. *Worldview in Christian perspective affirms the existence of the Trinitarian God whose essential character of love and justice*

---

30 Augustine, *Teaching Christianity: De Doctrina Christiana, The Works of St. Augustine for the 21st Century*, vol. 11, intro., trans., notes Edmund Hill (Hyde Park, NY: New City Press, 1996), 159–60 (§2.60).

establishes the moral order of the universe and whose Word, wisdom, and law define and govern all aspects of created existence. God is the ultimate reality whose Trinitarian nature, essential character, moral excellence, wonderful works, and sovereign rule constitute the objective reference point for all of reality. As a construct ontologically grounded in God himself, the nuance of objectivity is built into worldview from a Christian perspective.

Issues of subjectivity. In its philosophic history, *worldview* has also been understood in subjectivist terms as an individual's particular interpretation of life. As cognitive, affective, and volitional beings, all people by necessity must understand, care about, and act in the world. Christian theology would agree, recognizing this to be the operation of the heart. *Worldview in Christian perspective affirms that human beings as God's image and likeness are anchored and integrated in the heart as the subjective sphere of consciousness, which is decisive for shaping a vision of life and fulfilling the function typically ascribed to the notion of* worldview. Life proceeds "kardioptically," out of "a vision of the heart." That, I propose, is basically what a worldview is. I will develop this thesis in a bit more detail shortly.

Issues of sin and spiritual warfare. People are in a fallen condition, however. They suppress the truth in unrighteousness and manufacture surrogate deities and errant perspectives on the world. *Worldview in Christian perspective, therefore, implies the catastrophic effects of sin on the human heart, resulting in the fabrication of false, idolatrous belief systems in place of God and the engagement of the human race in cosmic spiritual warfare in which the truth about reality and the meaning of life are at stake.* There is no way out of this spiritual, intellectual, and moral destitution apart from the grace of God.

Issues of grace and redemption. The merciful character of God and his redemptive work are the central elements in biblical thought. *Worldview in Christian perspective affirms the gracious inbreaking of the kingdom of God into human history in the person and work of Jesus Christ who atones for sin, defeats the principalities and powers, and enables those who believe in him to obtain a knowledge of the true God as the creator, judge, and savior of the whole cosmos.* This kind of salvific transaction is wholly transformative in converting believers to God and renewing their perspectives on the whole of reality by truth. The formation of a Christian worldview, therefore, is ultimately a function of God's saving grace.

Thus, the implications of a divinely grounded objectivity, the reality of a heart-based human subjectivity, along with the themes of sin and spiritual warfare, grace and redemption, are the inferences built into the notion of worldview in a Christian context.

Let me return now to the issue of subjectivity in this Christian re-flection on worldview. The point I wish to emphasize is that the biblical teaching about the centrality of the "heart" in human life is a key to defining the notion of *worldview*. Theologian Gordon Spykman states, "the *imago Dei* embraces our entire selfhood in all its variegated func-tions centered and unified in the heart." Similarly, Karl Barth affirms that "the heart is not merely *a* but *the* reality of man, both wholly of soul and wholly of body."[31]

These theological claims about the heart as the core of the person are supported by the 1,000 or so instances (855 OT; 150 NT) in which the Scriptures in both the Old and New Testaments teach that it is the seat and source of the intellect, affections, will, and spirituality, as the loca-tion where we think, feel, choose, and worship. Proverbs 4:23 and 27:19 state respectively that "from the heart flow the springs of life," and that "the heart of man reflects man." Jesus supports this perspective, stating in Matthew 6:21 that what a person values most as one's treasure in life resides in the heart. In Luke 6:43–45, he adds that from the heart flow all of our deeds and words, for "The good man out of the good treasure of his heart brings forth what is good; and the evil man out of the evil treasure of his heart brings forth what is evil; for his mouth speaks from that which fills his heart." St. Paul prayed that "the eyes of the heart" would be enlightened so that believers might understand the magnitude of their callings in Christ (Ephesians 1:18). Thus, in the Old and New Testaments, for the Savior, and in the teaching of the Apostle Paul, the heart is the cornerstone of human existence.

On the basis of this biblical doctrine of the heart, I would like to make three suggestions about the concept of worldview. *First, I propose that the heart and its content, as the center of human consciousness, create and consti-tute what we commonly refer to as a worldview.* What the heart is and does in a biblical way is what the philosophers were getting at in various ways, though unconsciously, in devising and using the concept of worldview. Biblically speaking, then, life proceeds kardioptically, out of a vision of the heart, and that is what I think a worldview is! It is a vision of the heart, which is "our deepest organ of communication with the nature of things."[32]

---

31   Gordon J. Spykman, *Reformational Theology: A New Paradigm for Doing Dogmat-ics* (Grand Rapids: Eerdmans, 1992), 227; Karl Barth, *Church Dogmatics*, trans. Harold Knight, J. K. S. Reid, and R. H. Fuller (Edinburgh: T. and T. Clark, 1960), III/2, p. 436.

32   William James, "Is Life Worth Living," in *The Will to Believe and Other Essays in Popular Philosophy* (New York, c. 1896; reprint, New York: Dover, 1956), 62; quoted in

It is a vision of God, the universe, our world, and ourselves—rooted and grounded in the human heart. The heart of the matter of worldview is that worldview is a matter of the heart, with its deeply embedded ideas, its profound affections, its life-determining choices, and its essential religion. For according to its specific disposition, it grinds its own "lenses," metaphorically speaking, through which it perceives the world and life within it. As a function of the heart, therefore, *Weltanschauung* is an existential concept, indeed, a biblical concept, essential to human identity as the image and likeness of God.

Second, things that enter into the heart shape its vision of things, forming the basic assumptions upon which life proceeds. Before the springs flow *out of* the heart as a way of life, something must first and continue to flow into it to form a perspective on the world. Things are internalized *before* they are externalized. What the heart *receives* determines what it eventually *conceives.* What influences, then, shape a heart and determine its image of life? Certainly one's natural genetic inheritance, native personality traits, and inborn insights are critical components of the heart's composition. It is also deeply influenced by the manifold experiences of life. From early on, a torrential amount of content is poured into the reservoir of the heart from seemingly unlimited sources of varying quality, some of it pure, some of it polluted.[33] Once the powerful forces of both nature and nurture have shaped the content and dispositions of a heart, they comprise the "presuppositional basis of life."[34]

Presuppositions "… refer us," says Ted Peters, "to our fundamental vision of reality and the self-evident truths which are tacitly acknowledged in everything we comprehend and assert."[35] And as Michael Polanyi observes, when we acknowledge a set of presuppositions as an interpretative framework

---

William J. Wainwright, *Reason and the Heart: A Prolegomena to Passional Reason* (Ithaca, NY: Cornell University, 1995), 97.

33   I think here of these lines from singer/song writer Kate Campbell in the chorus to her song, "How Much Can One Heart Hold?" (*Monuments*, 2002, Large River Music).

How much can one heart hold,
A pound of dirt or a pound of gold,
We may never know the truth be told
How much can one heart hold.

34   A felicitous expression I heard in a lecture by David Aikman at The Oxbridge Conference sponsored by the C. S. Lewis Foundation in the summer of 1998, celebrating the centennial of the birth of C. S. Lewis. Here is a definition of a presupposition based on its etymology: *pre-sub-ponere* = that which is posited (believed) underneath (taken for granted) in advance (a priori).

35   Ted Peters, "The Nature and Role of Presupposition: An Inquiry into Contemporary Hermeneutics," *International Philosophical Quarterly* 14 (June 1974): 210.

for life, "we may be said to dwell in them as we do in our own body."[36]

In any case, the heart sustains an *interactive* or *reciprocal* relationship with the external world and, in the process, obtains an underlying vision of life, though it is difficult to explain exactly how it all happens.[37] In this dynamic process, basic assumptions are either ignored or discovered, followed, confirmed, challenged, put in crisis, reaffirmed, replaced, and solidified as the individual clings to a first, second, third "naïveté"—or even more—until death. Thus, worldviews are always works in progress. The proverbial warning to watch over the heart, therefore, could not be more prudent.

Third, the things that proceed out of the heart as a way of life reflect its true worldview. The best test to determine what vision of life truly grips a heart is to examine one's basic "conversation" in the world, to employ an antique term from the King's English. Truth claims and professed beliefs may or may not correspond with one's actual way of life. One's actual way of life may or may not correspond to one's truth claims or professed beliefs. If there is agreement, there is integrity. If there is not, there is hypocrisy. In any case, concrete behavior is a clear indicator of true belief, and whatever true beliefs reside in the heart and form its vision is what will show up in real life. Therefore, examine a person carefully (perhaps even yourself): listen to her speak, watch her act, observe her attitudes, detect her beliefs, and, in a short while, you will be led back to the tap root of her life in the basic assumptions of the heart that supply her with her genuine conception and way of life—ideas, beliefs, and words to the contrary notwithstanding.

Now this concept of worldview as a vision of the heart as I have articulated it here and in my book is acceptable as far as it goes. But now I think it needs to be augmented. Though this description has a strong existential thrust, I detect a lingering Cartesianism in my formulation in which the heart as the psychic center of the human person still remains a somewhat disembodied and independent thing that thinks, feels, wills, and worships. With the help of Michael Polanyi, mediated through the recent capable work of Esther Lightcap Meeks, I have recognized that this heart needs to be rooted in the physical body and this "enhearted" body or embodied heart needs to be anchored in the ebb and flow of the real world.

---

36   Michael Polanyi, *Personal Knowledge: Towards a Post-Critical Philosophy* (Chicago: University of Chicago, 1958, 1962), 60.
37   William James, *A Pluralistic Universe* (New York: Longmans, Green, and Company, 1925), 13.

God not only made the heart, but also the body, as he also made the world, and there is a divinely ordained coherence that unites them. Not only is there a bodily basis of all thought, as Polanyi taught, but the most basic way of being in and accessing the world is through the body. Worldviews grow out of lived bodily experience, and it is from their embodied situations that people decipher the world in felt semiotic, narratival, rational, epistemic, and hermeneutical ways. This basic way of being in the world through the heart-body unity constitutes a worldview.

This bodily based world consciousness is something of which most people are not typically cognizant, since it is an object of subsidiary, rather than of focal awareness, to employ Polanyian categories once again. Just as the body is not the object of direct attention in its daily operations, neither is there conscious awareness of worldview assumptions, which constitute a vision of life. Instead, both are indwelt tacitly. As Polanyi states, "when we accept a certain set of pre-suppositions and use them as our interpretative framework, we may be said to indwell them as we do in our own body. . . . As they are themselves our ultimate framework, they are essentially inarticulable."[38] Normally, people are as unconscious of their worldviews as they are of their bodies, unless both become the object of purposeful examination. Learning what it is like to live in a body tacitly is a helpful step in learning what it is like to have a worldview, and vice versa.[39] Thus, this world-oriented, bodily based, heart-centered understanding of worldview may provide a more complete picture and may do greater justice to an overall biblical anthropology.

There are two additional points that figure prominently in my concept of a worldview that merit very brief consideration. These are their semiotic and narrative character. In light of Umberto Eco's argument that the whole of culture must and can be studied as a semiotic phenomenon;[40] given the fact that a defining trait of humans as *imago Dei* who possess *logos* is the ability to use one thing to stand for another thing, especially in the form of letters, words, speech, and written discourse; and because Scripture teaches that the entire universe should be conceived pansemiotically and interpreted as a sign of God and his glorious power (e.g., Psalm 19:1): it seemed wise to examine the nature and function of worldview

---

38 Polanyi, *Personal Knowledge*, 60.

39 Esther L. Meek, "Working Implications of the Subsidiary Nature of Worldviews," a paper presented at the Midwest Regional Evangelical Theological Society Conference, Lincoln Christian College, 19 March 2004. See also Esther Lightcap Meek, *Longing to Know: The Philosophy of Knowledge for Ordinary People* (Grand Rapids: Brazos, 2003).

40 Umberto Eco, *A Theory of Semiotics, Advances in Semiotics* (Bloomington: Indiana University, 1976), 22.

sub specie semiotica. St. Augustine was also a catalyst in this regard in his demonstration of the role and power of signs in the process of communication and the acquisition of knowledge. As he states forthrightly in his *De Doctrina Christiana,* "Things are learned about through signs," and, in this magisterial treatise, he recognizes clearly that semiotic systems and symbolic worlds of various kinds are at the heart of the human drama insofar as they convey either the wine of truth or of error.

My suggestion is that there is a certain set or string of symbols that present the meaning of life and possess unique cultural power. These are rightly designated as "worldview." As an individual's or a culture's foundation and system of meaning, they are promulgated through countless communicative avenues and mysteriously find their way to the innermost regions of the embodied heart that resides in the world. They inform the categories of consciousness that define human existence and provide an interpretation and way of life. They are the putative object of faith, the basis for hope, and the essential source of individual and sociocultural security.

More often than not, and this is the second point, they have been formulated, received, and indwelt as a set of narratives or stories that establish a particular outlook on life. Semiotically constituted human beings in want of a solution to the riddles of the universe primarily fulfill this need in their trademark activity of telling stories that form a symbolic world for which people are inclined to live and even die. The power of stories to establish a context for life has been recognized since time immemorial by the traditions' greatest thinkers.

These stories that establish a symbolic world do indeed guide all forms of human activity. Worldview narratives create a particular kind of "mind" and serve in a normative fashion as "controlling stories."[41] The most fundamental stories associated with a *Weltanschauung*—those closest to its metaphysical, epistemological, and ethical epicenter—possess a kind of finality as the ultimate interpretation of reality in all its multifaceted aspects. Such stories are considered sacred, and they provide the adhesive that unites those who believe in them into a society characterized by shared perspectives and a common way of life. They also provide a tenacious grid by which competing narratives and alternative claims to truth are judged. Controlling stories, therefore, function in a regulatory

---

41   N. T. Wright, *The New Testament and the People of God* (Philadelphia: Fortress, 1992), 41–42. Wright acknowledges that the idea of "controlling stories" is derived from Nicholas Wolterstorff's concept of "control beliefs," which he discusses in his *Reason within the Bounds of Religion,* 2nd ed. (Grand Rapids: Eerdmans, 1984), 67.

fashion both positively and negatively and are able to bind those who accept them into an intellectual or spiritual commonwealth. Thus, the bulk of human praxis does seem to be under the jurisdiction of a worldview, including the significant activities of reasoning, interpreting, and knowing.

Philosophical Implications

Worldview and rationality. What is rational? What influence, if any, does a worldview have upon the operation and content of reason? Is rationality free from or dependent upon a worldview framework? Is there an "arch" or "olympian" kind of rationality transcending worldviews that is the same for all?[42] Or is what is reasonable worldview-dependent?

Three questions will illustrate the precise thrust of this inquiry regarding the relation of worldview and rationality. First, are the beliefs of primitive cultures less "rational" than those of the modern, scientific West? Second, in the conflict between Jews, Greeks, and Christians regarding the credibility of the New Testament gospel, with which party does rationality side? Third, do human beings manifest the utmost in rational virtue when they insist that for a proposition to be true, it must be a part of the noetic structure of strong foundationalism?

These questions and their answers reflect intense debates among anthropologists about what constitutes *cultural rationality*; among Jews, Gentiles, and Christians concerning *religious rationality*; and among philosophers over *epistemic rationality*. These differences make one thing clear: what is reasonable or what constitutes rationality is dependent upon prior commitments. What a person deems to be rational or irrational appears to be a function of the reasoner's worldview.

This is not to suggest that the actual laws of logic are altered by cultural context or philosophic orientation. The laws of noncontradiction, identity, and excluded middle are, indeed, universal. The content, however, with which these laws of logic function, is markedly different. In Aristotelian terms, the formal cause of rationality is the same, but its material cause may vary considerably. Bare reason is embarrassed by nakedness and always seeks to be clothed in a worldview tradition.

Recently, Alasdair MacIntyre has supported this contention that rationality is rooted in various historical traditions. His concern in *Whose*

---

42 The idea of an "arch-rationalism" as an absolutist style of reason is from Ian Hacking, "Language, Truth and Reason," in *Rationality and Relativism*, ed. Martin Hollis and Steven Lukes (Cambridge, MA: MIT, 1982), 51–53; the notion of "olympian reason" as a reasoning process from a "god's eye point of view" is from Herbert Simon, *Reason in Human Affairs* (Stanford: Stanford University, 1983), 34–35.

Justice? Which Rationality? is, of course, on moral matters, in particular the conception of justice. In his investigation, however, he recognized that rival conceptions of justice presupposed rival conceptions of rationality. The Enlightenment's attempt to formulate an objective view of reason that could adjudicate this matter failed. Thus, MacIntyre takes the discussion to a deeper level and argues for a conception of rational inquiry that is embodied in a tradition. The rationality of doctrines has to be understood in terms of historical context. For this reason, MacIntyre asserts, there are "rationalities rather than [a] rationality."[43] At the end of the day, he seems to be saying that the questions about "whose justice" and "which rationality" is a matter intimately related to worldview. As he puts it, "it has become evident that *conceptions of justice and of practical rationality generally and characteristically confront us as closely related aspects of some larger, more or less well-articulated, overall view of human life and of its place in nature.*"[44]

If MacIntyre's analysis stands, then it seems prudent to assert that what is deemed to be rational is dependent on a larger frame of reference in which the perceived logic of the universe inheres. A fundamental outlook on life determines how the saw of reason itself cuts. Along these lines, let me state unequivocally my conviction that the true cosmic rationality resides in the Trinitarian God and his graciously revealed, infallible Word.

Worldview and hermeneutics. The goal of modern thinkers was to design an objective method of understanding that circumvents the problem of the hermeneutic circle in which the meaning of texts is determined in advance by the scholars' *aprioris.* Their goal was to move as far away from interpretation as possible in hopes of obtaining scientific certitude. Why fool around with values when facts will do?

This separation of knowledge and interpretation, however, seems naïve, unrealistic, and self-referentially incoherent: *naïve* in its view of human nature, *unrealistic* in its expectation of a self-dispossessed objectivity, and *incoherent* in its establishment of a prejudice against prejudice. As Hans-Georg Gadamer famously points out, "There is one prejudice of the Enlightenment that defines its essence: the fundamental prejudice of the Enlightenment is the prejudice against prejudice itself, which denies tradition its power."[45]

---

43 Alasdair MacIntyre, *Whose Justice? Which Rationality?* (Notre Dame: University of Notre Dame, 1988), 9.
44 MacIntyre, *Whose Justice?* 389 (emphasis added).
45 Hans-Georg Gadamer, *Truth and Method*, 2nd rev. ed., trans. Joel Weinsheimer and

The Enlightenment's effort at stamping out all question-begging traditions became the new question-begging tradition of modernity. The intention to escape human subjectivity and its hermeneutic influence by means of the objectivity of science failed. In the contest, then, between Enlightenment objectivism and the hermeneutic circle, the latter, as postmodern critics have gleefully pointed out, triumphed over the former. The process of interpretation, like reason, is guided by prejudices and is tradition bound. As Rudolph Bultmann (1884–1976) affirms, "there cannot be any such thing as exegesis without presuppositions."[46] It is influenced significantly, according to the present argument, by worldview.

Both Martin Heidegger and Hans-Georg Gadamer critique this Enlightenment objectivist position by reconnecting humanity to being, history, and the world.[47] This reimmersion into the stream of human experience effectively eliminated the possibility of a "God's eye point of view" in all attempts to explain the nature of things immaculately. Therefore, no one is an interpretative island existing independently as a purely rational hermeneutic entity. The modern image of the solitary individual divested of self-interest in a scientific pursuit of objective knowledge of the world stands in contrast to the communitarian ideals of the premodern and postmodern periods. In both of these eras, the power of history and a narrative tradition to shape consciousness is recognized, along with its hermeneutic implications.[48] Comprehension of things does not take place in a vacuum, but in social, historical, and linguistic contexts.

This raises the most important question, however, in the matter of relating hermeneutics and worldview, which is whether any final meaning is possible. The answer, so it seems, depends on one's worldview! If both God and humanity are dead—the two original sources of hermeneutical meaning, taking the cosmos with them and leaving nothing in their place—then we are left with nothing but pointless talk. As Stanley Rosen affirms, "If nothing is real, the real is nothing; there is no difference between the written lines of a text and the blank spaces between them."[49]

Donald G. Marshall (New York: Continuum, 1993), 270.

46 Rudolph Bultmann, "Is Exegesis Without Presuppositions Possible?" in *New Testament and Mythology and Other Basic Writings*, selected, ed. trans., Schubert M. Ogden (Philadelphia: Fortress, 1984), 146.

47 Martin Heidegger, *Being and Time*, trans. John Macquarrie and Edward Robinson (New York: Harper and Row, 1962).

48 Anthony C. Thiselton, *New Horizons in Hermeneutics: The Theory and Practice of Transforming Biblical Reading* (Grand Rapids: Zondervan, 1992), 143.

49 Stanley Rosen, *Hermeneutics as Politics*, Odéon (New York: Oxford University, 1987), 161.

On the other hand, as George Steiner points out, God's existence changes everything hermeneutically. A universe derived from and ordered by the Logos of God is the foundation and reference point by which to interpret the world truthfully. As Steiner puts it in his book *Real Presences*, "the wager on the meaning of meaning . . . is a wager on transcendence."[50]

Thus, not only is the art and science of interpretation affected by a worldview, but the question about the very possibility of meaning itself is also worldview dependent. The question hinges on the decision between the antithetical worldviews of atheism or theism. For if there is no God, there is no final meaning, but if there is, it makes all of the difference in the world. God and his Word constitute the world's true hermeneutic.

Worldview and epistemology. If the presence of a worldview affects reasoning and interpreting in significant ways, then what kind of effect does it have on the process of knowing itself? When it comes to worldview and knowledge, are its adherents connected with reality or just their view of it? Or is it perhaps a little bit of both? Three views are commonly recognized in responding to this query.

Naïve or *common-sense realism* argues that comprehension of the cosmos is direct and accurate, substantially unaffected by worldview presuppositions or any other person-relative influences. *Critical realism* posits an objectively existing world and the possibility of trustworthy knowledge of it. But it also recognizes the prejudices that inevitably accompany human knowing and demands an ongoing critical conversation about the essentials of one's outlook. *Creative antirealism* is a view positing a radical disjunction between what is actually there and the many creative views of it. Worldviews in this context are all there are, belief systems that are reified and sustain no necessary connection to reality as such.

I submit that *critical realism* is the most responsible position in judging between these three options relating worldview and knowledge. This viewpoint avoids the dogmatism and arrogance of modernity and the skepticism and despair of postmodernity. Rather, it promotes a sensible view of human knowledge marked by both epistemic confidence and humility. It is a golden mean epistemology that seeks to avoid the excesses and deficiencies of its competitors.

There is, therefore, no view from nowhere! All things are known from somewhere! Depending upon where one stands will determine whether things are obscured or clarified. As C. S. Lewis says in *The Magician's Nephew*, "For what you see and hear depends a good deal on where

---

50   George Steiner, *Real Presences* (Chicago: University of Chicago, 1989), 4.

you are standing: it also depends on what sort of person you are."[51]

There is, therefore, a persistent need for interaction with other perspectives to challenge and certify our take on the nature of things. I see things in my framework that you do not see; you see things in your framework that I do not see. I see and point out your shortcomings; you see and point out my shortcomings. Through these respective contributions and mutual criticisms, through the exercise of what Russian literary critic Mikhail Bakhtin calls a "dialogical imagination," the desideratum is an ever-increasing understanding of reality.[52] At least in part, knowledge about the world is the fruit of a dialectical process rooted in a great conversation that ultimately must take its cue from the Greatest Conversation between God and humanity rooted in Scripture, which is the world's and the Church's true truth.

Conclusion

A worldview, then, constitutes the symbolic universe that has profound implications on a variety of significant human practices. It digs the channels in which the waters of reason flow. It establishes the hermeneutic framework by which texts are interpreted. It is that mental medium through which the world is known. Human life in its variegated aspects, so it seems, proceeds kardioptically out of a vision of an embodied heart living in the world. Theologically speaking, to get that vision right requires a gracious work of the sovereign, Trinitarian God who has revealed himself as the creator, judge, and redeemer of the world. This big biblical picture of the Christian faith as a comprehensive, coherent, and vivifying interpretation of all aspects of life was preeminently attractive and relevant to astute thinkers like James Orr and Abraham Kuyper and their worldview disciples. They and their followers introduced this larger, worldview way of apprehending the Christian faith into the culture and history of the evangelical Church. Thus the history, theology, and implications of this notion of worldview serve to confirm my intuitive attraction to G. K. Chesterton's conviction "that the most practical and important thing about a person is still his view of the universe."

---

51   C. S. Lewis, *The Magician's Nephew* (New York: Macmillan, Collier Books, 1955, 1970), 125.
52   Mikhail M. Bakhtin, *Speech Genres and Other Late Essays*, trans. Vern W. McGee, ed. Caryl Emerson and Michael Holquist (Austin: University of Texas, 1986), 7.

Response to David Naugle

MICHAEL STEVENS

Thank you, David, for the important work you have done, from which this presentation tonight extends. One of the best decisions we have made in faculty development here at Cornerstone was to set up groups last year to read and discuss your book *Worldview: The History of a Concept*. Especially helpful and challenging to us were your mini-treatises on the history of worldview discourse in the various academic disciplines.

This paper builds upon your historical survey at a crucial juncture, where you have begun to distill what the Reformed and then the evangelical traditions have done with the totalizing notion of *Weltanschauung*.

A question that hovers at the periphery of the first part of your paper regards how much the combative historical moment and the constraints felt by such thinkers as Orr, Henry, Clark, and even Schaeffer have permanently biased evangelical thinking about worldview in the direction of apologetics. It might be the case that Kuyper's *Stone Lectures* leave little space for other directions. You make allusion to the question of the "suitability" of worldview thinking for the Church, suggesting a more organic space within in the Body of Christ—but this is, perhaps, just the question you and others will be fleshing out as you speak in churches and seminaries on the notion of the "worldview-driven church."

If I may concentrate on the second half of your paper, I would like to pull out several striking images/metaphors/analogies (who selected all of these English and Rhetoric instructors as respondents, by the way?) that both persuade and yet might bear further unpacking.

First, you make mention of your key project, whereby worldview might be "regenerated and baptized in biblical waters, cleansing it of modern and postmodern impurities," then back this up with St. Augustine's own analogy of the "Egyptian gold." Now, our mutual Baptist institutional heritages notwithstanding, let me ask how efficacious such a "baptism" as you suggest can really be? Can the very motives for adoption of a totalizing framework be overhauled and the seeming "original sin," which you trace back at least to Kant, be finally washed away?

Second, your placing of worldview in the deep core of the human heart (this "kardioptics" you speak of) seems perhaps your most profound and resonant image, yet its ambiguities are also potentially problematic. You mention the heart "grinding its own lenses" under the auspices of "the powerful forces of both nature and nurture"—all of which seems right—but where then does the philosophical enterprise enter in? How does the life of the mind fit? Does the proliferation of Spiritual Formation offices on Christian college campuses—and the hybrid notions of a thinker like Dallas Willard—indicate that worldview formation is a task of *kardia* and maybe *psuche*, but not clearly of *nous*?

Third, I love your image of stories, especially sacred stories, forming in us a "tenacious grid" by which to judge truth claims. This allows me to get back to the issue of the Church (especially the local Body) and, more fundamentally, the family as the location of worldview formation. How might we in the academy better attend to those prime dispensaries of story? And how do you see our task in Christian higher education fitting into this "grid-making," especially with reference to Cal Seerveld's notion of a worldview having potential to be realized in a "world and life vision"?

Finally, can there be a "golden mean" between "the dogmatism and arrogance of modernity, and the skepticism and despair of postmodernity" that would not serve to dislocate the Christian vision from time and place and particularity? With this fundamental difficulty, and also with exceeding praise for the work you have done in setting the context for just such discussions, I leave you the floor to respond.

Part II
Concern and Critique:
Christian Worldview and Postmodernity

Evangelicals and Worldview Confusion

GEORGE N. PIERSON

My original intention for this essay was to show that the concept of *worldview* has been misused by both traditional orthodox evangelicals and more unorthodox postmodern evangelicals. The former have uncritically embraced truth and certainty; the latter usually dismissed these as holdovers from modernity. The former were overly confident, while the latter were overly skeptical. But the scope of such a study was too large for this volume. Therefore, I will focus on the orthodox evangelicals, arguing that today many such evangelical scholars misunderstand and, therefore, misuse the concept of worldview in two ways.[1] First, they unwittingly end up with a concept of worldview that has within it inner tensions and contradictions. Second, some evangelicals leave out or blithely pass over issues essential to the historically responsible use of worldview, issues that, if they are going to use worldview, they at least ought to acknowledge, if not address.

More specifically, I plan to show that evangelicals adopt some *but not all* of the associated concepts that the fathers of the contemporary notion of Christian worldview, Abraham Kuyper and Herman Dooyeweerd, developed.[2] And the concepts that are left out are exactly those that make

---

1 Awareness of this problem may be gradually increasing. James Sire, in his recent book *Naming the Elephant: Worldview as a Concept* comments that part of his reason for writing the book was his "own growing sense of dissatisfaction with the cursory way I have dealt with the concept of worldview. The definition in the first three editions of *The Universe Next Door* now seems inadequate to me" (Downers Grove: InterVarsity, 2004, p. 13).

2 See, for example, Abraham Kuyper, *Lectures on Calvinism* (Grand Rapids: Eerdmans, 1931) and Herman Dooyeweerd, *A New Critique of Theoretical Thought* (Philadelphia: Presbyterian and Reformed, 1958). David Naugle, in his *Worldview: The History of a Concept* (Grand Rapids: Eerdmans, 2002) makes a strong historical case that the term

the concept of worldview distinctive and biblical. This happens, as far as I can tell, without most evangelicals even being aware of what has been left out. These evangelical scholars appear unfamiliar with the full-orbed concept of worldview as it was developed by Kuyper and Dooyeweerd. David Naugle's *Worldview: The History of a Concept* is a needed corrective to these tendencies, but it does not go far enough.[3] It is my contention that while one need not follow every step taken by Kuyper, Dooyeweerd, and others, one ought at least to explain why one has appropriated Kuyper's and Dooyeweerd's notion of worldview without appropriating the rich conceptual framework that these two thinkers believed to be ineluctably linked to it.

The result is that while evangelicals use worldview as though it were a new concept, what they name by it is often either some traditional sort of Christian philosophy or some moral systematics. In most cases, these traditional positions stand in tension to or at odds with the fuller meaning of worldview to which they selectively appeal. Second, even when the use of worldview is aimed at improving upon or even superseding the more traditional Christian philosophical/moral systematics, the effort falls flat because some key elements of weakness in the traditional views are not addressed. Some examples of what many evangelicals leave out are a) the nature of the limitations of reason (Is this due to sin or finitude?); b) the goodness of creation and the reality of the fall (Is creation characterized by antithetical conflict or redemptive harmony?); and c) the way in which creation is knowable and known (Is all knowing rational? How does everyday experience, also of faith, contribute to knowing?) I will show that these issues are not addressed by most evangelicals, even though the positive and historically responsible use of worldview, in fact, demands that these and other areas be acknowledged. In other words, what I am proposing is that if the use of the concept of worldview is advocated by evangelicals because it offers new and distinctive insight, then the concept should really *be* distinctive and not be turned into just a new name for familiar old concepts. And since what is actually and genuinely distinctive about worldview is largely the work of Kuyper and Dooyeweerd, then evangelicals ought to recognize these distinctives. This, I believe, will broaden the scope of the concept to include a Christian critique

---

worldview has come into the evangelical vocabulary largely through these two sources.

3   Naugle's work, while excellent in presenting the nineteenth- and early nineteenth-century German philosophical background to *Weltanschauung*, gives far less coverage to the unique development of *Weltanschauung* by Herman Dooyeweerd, Herman Bavinck, and Dirk Vollenhoven, just to name a few. As a result, some of the most formative reflection on a Christian use of *Weltanschauung* goes largely unremarked.

of reason, knowing, and the nature of creation and creation order.

To this end, I have selected four problem areas that are representative of the common evangelical use of worldview. They are 1) the failure to distinguish between theoretical and pretheoretical human experience; 2) the failure to recognize the distinction between structure and direction (with implications for misunderstanding of the fall and the antithesis); 3) the failure to recognize the completely religious nature of all of life; and 4) the failure to distinguish between normativity and morality.[4]

The Distinction Between Theoretical and Pretheoretical Thought

Possibly the most common evangelical misuse of worldview is the conflation of worldview and philosophy and/or worldview and theology. This produces statements to the effect that your worldview is a *system* of specific beliefs and therefore subject to norms of formal logical orderliness for philosophical and/or theological systems. Thus, for example, Charles Colson and Nancy Pearcey, in their *How Now Shall We Live?*, describe how worldviews "form a grid that we can use to break down the *inner logic* of every belief *system* or philosophy that we encounter . . . ."[5] James Sire observes that "both in the works of most Christian worldview analysts—such as James Orr, James Olthuis, Arthur Holmes and Ronald Nash—and my own *Universe Next Door*, worldview is first described in intellectual terms, such as 'system of beliefs,' 'set of presuppositions' or 'conceptual scheme.'"[6]

Even when the claims are not so explicit, the context of what is said often implies that worldviews are formal systems of thought. One example is found in the materials that come out of the Worldview Academy of Bryan, Texas, which conducts "Worldview Leadership Camps" around the country for young people. Their *Student Notebook*, after a brief introduction to worldviews, focuses on thinking as the way to understand biblical truth,[7] but in case anyone is unclear about what "thinking" means, this section is followed by two pages of "Common Informal

---

4   I would suggest that other areas that should be addressed would include the uncritical use of the notion of the *analogia entis*; the need for a deeper analysis of the right understanding of, and relationship between epistemology and ontology; and a fresh look at a Biblical idea of truth.

5   Charles Colson and Nancy Pearcey, *How Now Shall We Live?* (Wheaton: Tyndale House, 1999), 14 (emphasis added).

6   Sire, *Naming the Elephant*, 100–1. Sire adds that "I now want to ask whether this is quite accurate" (ibid.). See also page 91. Naugle, *Worldviews*, provides some additional examples on pages 14, 338.

7   Worldview Academy of Bryan, *Student Notebook* (Bryan, TX: Worldview Academy, 1998), 17.

Fallacies."[8] In a similar vein, the section that addresses eight specific areas where our culture calls for worldview discernment is titled "Apologetics/ Evangelism."[9]

My concern here is that these authors seem to presuppose the primacy and priority of formal abstract thought. By contrast, worldview, both in its use by Wilhelm Dilthey[10] and its elaboration by Kuyper[11] and Dooyeweerd, was developed to account for what Michael Polanyi would call tacit dimensions and what Dooyeweerd before him would call naïve pretheoretical experience.[12] We know more than we can express formally; sometimes our deepest and richest knowings cannot be fully said or formalized. Examples abound: I know that I love my wife; I know that my redeemer lives; I know what appropriate "social space" is in our culture; I know that the Bible is absolutely trustworthy and true—the list goes on.[13]

As a scholar, I could produce a scholarly (i.e., theoretical) explanation of these sorts of human experiences. But these experiences can be legitimate forms of knowing *without such a theoretical formal account being available*, as the above biblical allusion from Job 19:25 implies. Pretheoretical knowing has its own kind of legitimacy, as does theoretical knowing. This is a more phenomenological way of saying what I believe Nicholas Wolterstorff and Alvin Plantinga have been saying more analytically in their critique of foundationalism—that certain knowings are properly basic and properly legitimate without being logically demonstrable.[14] Both the pretheoretical *and* the theoretical are ways of knowing. But while the pretheoretical can happen without the theoretical, the converse is not the case. Theoretical activity is always rooted in pretheoretical everyday experience with its integral and largely seamless web of experience.[15] Standing in the latter, theoretical activity proceeds

---

8   Worldview Academy, *Student Notebook* 18–19.

9   Worldview Academy, *Student Notebook* 41.

10   Sire, *Naming*, 39.

11   See, for example, Kuyper, *Lectures on Calvinism*, 20, 24; Naugle, *Worldview*, 271–74.

12   Dooyeweerd, *New Critique*, I, 3, 34, 41–42. I will stay with Dooyeweerd's terminology in this paper, but his meaning could be preserved just as well by the term *nontheoretical*.

13   Naugle, *Worldview*, 271–74.

14   Nicholas Wolterstorff, *Reason Within the Bounds of Religion* (Grand Rapids: Eerdmans, 1976), Chap. 6; Alvin Plantinga, *Warranted Christian Belief* (New York: Oxford University, 2000), 172–73.

15   I am drawing on Dooyeweerd's work here (for example, *New Critique*, I, 43), but this sort of approach is common in phenomenological analysis.

to intentionally examine the distinct dimensions of God's good creation by separating them out from the pretheoretical unity of experience. For example, we together could experience the room in which I am writing these words pretheoretically as a unified whole, "the room." It is the theoretical attitude that can focus on the distinctive social or economic or rational or aesthetic or whatever aspects of this particular place.

Dooyeweerd called this latter theoretical attitude the *Gegenstand* relation;[16] it is more traditionally called objective knowing or theorizing, since theories are often produced by assessing a series of acts by which we "stand over against" the objects and draw from the experience an assertion about the overarching orderliness that they all exhibit. But the point here is that such theorizing is always secondary in the sense that it is only possible because humans are first pretheoretical knowers.

What makes worldview distinctive is its pretheoretical character. This means that our worldviews will exhibit a certain orderliness, but this orderliness need not be reduced to a formal objective rational or logical order, because rational or logical order (at least as we usually use the terms) is typically characteristic of theoretical activity and has reference to only this one sort of knowing. Thus, to speak of a worldview as a system is problematic at best, for "system" invokes rational orderliness of a theoretical kind. Now, any theoretical activity unavoidably will entail rationality (or articulable orderliness), and this is fine and necessary. But to speak of worldview as having this latter type of orderliness is to imply that worldview beliefs are not so much presupposed as they are inferred. Thinking this way results in a failure to recognize that while all worldviews involve presuppositions, not all presuppositions are worldviewish in nature.[17]

In a nutshell, this is one of the objections I have to aspects of the work of Cornelius Van Til, who, in turn, deeply influenced Francis Schaeffer, the first "worldview" thinker to whom people of my generation were often exposed. Although Van Til learned his presuppositionalism in

16   Dooyeweerd, *New Critique*, 6, 38–44.
17   Failure to see this distinction can also cause problems of a different nature. Greg Clark, in his chapter titled "The Nature of Conversion: How the Rhetoric of Worldview Philosophy Can Betray Evangelicals," accuses worldviewish thinking of replacing Jesus Christ with a set of correct propositions (*The Nature of Confession: Evangelicals and Liberals in Conversation*, ed. Timothy R. Phillips, and Dennis Okholm [Downers Grove: InterVarsity, 1996]). While doing such would certainly be deserving of Clark's criticism, he unfortunately only cites some of the evangelicals I have already mentioned as "worldviewish" thinkers, failing to see that these evangelicals are not using "worldview" soundly and that his criticism simply does not apply to the full-orbed approach to "worldview" coming out of Amsterdam.

Amsterdam,[18] he maintained (contrary to Dooyeweerd) that any world-view other than a biblical one was inherently irrational.[19] He would have been better served had he said that any worldview other than a biblical one is ultimately unable to produce a durable concept of order. We will revisit this issue again shortly when I address the difficult but essential concept of structure and direction.

What often results from assuming worldviews to be rational systems is that evangelicals conflate worldview with philosophy, which is more properly understood to be a theoretical discipline. Although none of the originators of the concept of worldview use it this way, it is easy to slip into this usage. The same can be said about the use of theology to refer to almost any statement about God and/or Scripture, a practice common to evangelicals. By this reckoning, the work of, say, John Calvin and the expressed Christian beliefs of a six-year-old child are both univocally the-ology. But this renders theology incomprehensible. The problem arises because evangelicals rightly want to acknowledge the role of faith in both Calvin and the child. But lacking a way to refer to faith knowing other than with the term *theology*, confusion occurs. And since biblical world-view embraces and expresses faith, worldview must be theology.

The problem dissolves, though, when it is recognized that faith is a way of being and knowing that is pretheoretical and, therefore, founda-tional to theology and everything else. Naturally, this pretheoretical state known as faith will make its presence known in any worldview. Not only is this the case phenomenologically, but there is strong biblical warrant for viewing faith this way, as Dooyeweerd and others have articulated. They speak of faith and religion as first pretheoretical or what they call "confes-sional"; that is, they acknowledge that the work of God in a heart by his Holy Spirit produces faith in a sense that is significantly beyond words.[20]

---

18 See, for example, Cornelius Van Til's response to Herman Dooyeweerd, in *Jerusalem and Athens: Critical Discussions on the Philosophy and Apologetics of Cornelius Van Til*, ed. E. R. Geehan (Phillipsburg: Presbyterian and Reformed, 1980), 89–127. Van Til makes numerous passing references to his reading of Bavinck, Kuyper, Dooyeweerd, and Vol-lenhoven.

19 See, for example, Van Til's "My Credo," in *Jerusalem and Athens*, 21. I bring in Van Til here not only because of his influence on Schaeffer, which carries down to today (Nancy Pearcey credits Schaeffer in a number of her works, including her latest, *Total Truth: Liberating Christianity from Its Cultural Captivity* [Wheaton: Crossway Books, 2004]), but also because Van Til seems to be influencing an increasing number of people associated with Doug Wilson and Peter Leithart of Moscow, Idaho. Their influence in the Christian home school and classical school movements has spread Van Tilian notions of the sort I cite to an increasingly wide and diverse evangelical audience.

20 An excellent summary of this issue can be found in Gordon Spykman, *Reformational*

The Completely Religious Nature of Life

When I was first exposed to worldview thinking, one of the phrases popular among our little group of zealots was "life is religion." The phrase has fallen out of favor, which is too bad. It is still a serviceable phrase because it reminds us of one of the central tenants of worldview thinking—that from the heart flow all of the issues of life (including one's worldview) and that the condition of one's heart, the allegiances of one's heart, are one's religion.[21] Evangelicals have little initial difficulty understanding Christian faith in this manner. Their problem comes when they are asked to view, for example, materialism or scientism as a religion. The problems are obvious—while scientism (the belief that *all* truth comes from scientific knowing alone) is a well-known enemy of evangelical faith, it does not have temples, hymns, priests, and so on. In fact, it denies that it is a religion. Moreover, evangelicals think, if we proceed to view scientism as a religion (and assuming we could get its practitioners to accept this designation), would not this result in unanticipated negative consequences—such as denying the objectivity of science (after all, is not water just H_2O for believer and unbeliever?) or giving scientism as much legitimacy as Christianity or other so-called "religions"?

We do well to go cautiously here, for in our day it is perilously easy to segue from a critique of scientism to a critique of science, from a critique of objectivism to a critique of objectivity. But I would still say we need critique here (albeit a cautious critique), because the evidence, both logical and phenomenological, is overwhelming that science properly done is necessarily rooted in pre-theoretical convictions that are ultimately religious in character. In other words, science is also a matter of faith. Moreover, recognizing the inherently religious nature of life is tremendously liberating for Christians (hence the popularity of the phrase "life is religion" thirty years ago) because it recognizes what many Christians sense existentially—that *all* of life is to be intimately connected to the love, worship, and service of God and that, absent this, sinful humanity will of necessity substitute something else for God. Your most basic beliefs show forth that to which you give ultimate allegiance. Said another way, to speak of worldview is to imply the central biblical role of the heart, which is that place where a spirit dwells and which is the seat

---

Theology: A New Paradigm for Doing Dogmatics (Grand Rapids: Eerdmans, 1992), Chap. V, sections 12, 13, and 19. His basic point (which he gets from Dooyeweerd) is that the old issue of whether theology or philosophy is queen of the sciences is a canard. Both are founded on *faith*, the pretheoretical experience of knowing Jesus Christ.

21   Roy Clouser, in his *Knowing With the Heart: Religious Experience and Belief in God* (Downers Grove: InterVarsity, 1999), makes this case, especially in Chaps. 1 and 2.

of religion.[22]

Many evangelicals have adopted the term *worldview* precisely because of their desire to live life more integrally, getting away from the traditional sacred-secular distinctions and living a faith that can address all aspects of life. Yet I suspect that they hesitate to say that "life is religion" because religion seems so, well, *spiritual,* and, after all, if Christianity is true, then it is more than just a religion (read "more than just subjective experience")—it is a system of timeless truth. Moreover, some probably fear that if religion is at the root of everything, including theology, then either theology is not the root of knowledge or theology is subjective and relative.

These are legitimate concerns, but they should not be ultimate concerns. Understanding "religious faith" as what we hold in our hearts as ultimate has the following advantages: it is how the Scriptures speak; it allows for a more complete phenomenological account of actual human behavior; it allows for a much-needed rethinking of a biblical notion of objectivity and truth; and it frees us from the still-pervasive sense among evangelicals that, for example, it is more spiritual to be a missionary than a biochemist. It also helps prevent evangelicals from reverting uncritically to some version of traditional apologetics, where religious faith is sometimes presented as though it consisted in the system of true propositions. There is a place for apologetics, including many aspects of traditional apologetics, but only if apologetics are understood within a more biblical epistemology and ontology. It is possible to critique objectivism and rationalism without necessarily ending up rejecting objectivity and rationality.

The Distinction Between Structure and Direction

In my estimation and that of some other Christian scholars, such as Al Wolters,[23] the distinction between structure and direction that flows out of the Kuyperian-Dooyeweerdian perspective is the most distinctive and original contribution to philosophical thought and worldview analy-

22 For some recent treatments of the importance of the Biblical notion of "heart," see Naugle, *Worldview,* 267–74, 345; Roy Clouser, *The Myth of Religious Neutrality: An Essay on the Hidden Role of Religious Belief in Theories* (Notre Dame: University of Notre Dame, 1991), 161–63, 240–41, and *Knowing With the Heart,* Chap. 4; and Sire, *Naming,* 123–24.

23 E-mail exchange, July, 2004. John H. Kok sheds further light on the origins of "structure-direction" in an unpublished paper titled "Runner and the Echo of Vollenhoven Thinking," in which he shows how H. Evan Runner, the late professor of philosophy at Calvin College who influenced a whole generation of his students to study Dooyeweerd and Vollenhoven, derived his use of "structure-direction" language from the various Dutch works of Vollenhoven.

sis to come from the Amsterdam school, yet it may be the least understood dimension of worldview thinking.[24] In a nutshell, "structure-direction" involves the claim that all of creation exhibits both enduring **structure**, i.e., God-given creation order, and, to one degree or another, right or wrong **direction**, i.e., responding to God's structure by either serving God to his glory or by rebellious sinfulness. The structure-direction distinction says that for any phenomenon in question it exists in such a way or functions in such a way (structure) that it either points toward God (rightly directed) or away from him (wrongly directed).[25]

This is really nothing more than a fresh way of addressing the age-old issue about which every thoughtful Christian reflects—how can creation be good and sin be real? The traditional tendency has been either to treat the created and physical as inherently fallen (hence, for example, some Christians' negative attitudes toward bodiliness and sexuality) or to limit the scope of the fall (so, for example, the will and the affections are fallen but the reason is essentially free from sin). In varying degrees both are still around today. For example, Sire, in *Naming the Elephant*, which is so good at advocating for a deeper understanding of worldview and heart, gets into difficulties here. In discussing why few have adopted Dooyeweerd's notion of the antithesis, i.e., the radicality of the conflict between righteousness and evil, Sire states that "the major reason, I think, is that there is such a large overlap between how Christians and non-Christians view reality that Dooyeweerd's radical antithesis between the Christian worldview and all others seems not to describe reality."[26] Sire assumes here that mis*direction* (which Kuyper and Dooyeweerd called "antithesis") must always produce false *structural* insights. And since unbelievers can have sound *structural* insights, "antithesis" does not describe reality. Said another way, Sire is claiming that the fruits of a heart directed sinfully against God do not affect every area of life.

I would turn the problem around and ask Sire and other evangelicals how they can explain the undeniable structural insights of many unbe-

---

24   As far as I can tell, the concept was first introduced to English-speaking audiences by Runner in books and lectures in the 1950s and 60s, but it is probably Al Wolters' use of "structure and direction" in *Creation Regained: Biblical Basics for a Reformational Worldview* (2nd ed. Grand Rapids: Eerdmans, 2005 [1985]), Chap. 4, that was the first reasonably developed use in English. See also footnote 23.

25   Some of the most accessible explanations of "structure-direction" are found in Wolters, Chap. 5, and Brian Walsh and Richard Middleton, *Transforming Vision: Shaping a Christian Worldview* (Downers Grove: InterVarsity, 1984), 88–90.

26   Sire, *Naming*, 87. The antithesis, as used by Dooyeweerd, is a *directional* phenomenon, something Sire fails to notice.

lievers while still affirming the biblical claim of the radicality of sin. As far as I can tell, it is only a full-orbed notion of worldview that can do this because it involves saying that one's most basic beliefs, one's faith, express a heart-indwelt spiritual condition and that this spiritual condition can act in such a way that even one's reason can have a (structural) soundness yet be producing distorted results (misdirection).[27] One's heart can make oneself do funny things.

Because of this misunderstanding, evangelical users of worldview have a hard time, for example, giving an epistemic account of an unbiblical presupposition, such as the ultimacy of the physical, often called naturalism. The problem is that very bright and logical people hold such beliefs quite (structurally) logically and apply their logic quite effectively in other areas, yet their naturalism is in error because it is unbiblical (misdirection). But if it is in error (misdirection), how can it be logical (good structure)?[28]

The Amsterdam school takes a fresh approach here, one evangelicals would do well to discover, by saying that *everything* is structurally good (there is nothing in creation that is not ordered/structured by God) and that everything, in varying degrees, is directionally bad (all of creation is fallen in sin) but redeemable (all of creation will be regained). This is usually captured in another Kuyperian-inspired phrase that is becoming commonplace among evangelicals, *creation-fall-redemption*.[29] My contention is that only structure-direction thinking can really explain what is implied in worldview analysis—that as sinners our most basic, heart-indwelt spiritual commitments, pretheoretical in character, are capable of twisting and distorting our God-given structures, especially our noetic structures, apart from Christ. Without this acknowledgment that the condition of the heart is capable of distorting and perverting the good structures of creation, many evangelicals end up maintaining that a biblical worldview is true and right because all of the others are (structurally) bad. The solution to the problem, then, becomes a rational assertion of the rational superiority of Christian thinking. When this falls short of explaining the phenomena of often very insightful yet unbelieving thinking, let alone convincing the unbelievers of their errors, evangelicals may fall back on saying that the heart is responsible (which is true) but they

27 See Wolters, *Creation Regained*, 78ff.; Clouser, Myth, 74–93.
28 This, I believe, is the fundamental problem in Van Til's approach.
29 Although they did not originate it, I believe that Walsh and Middleton's *Transforming Vision* and Wolters' *Creation Regained* were probably responsible for the wide dissemination among evangelicals of the *creation-fall-redemption* motif.

cannot really account for the root of the problem.

The Problem of the Moral and the Normative

One of the most distinctively evangelical ways of misappropriating worldview thinking is the conflation of moral order with cosmic order. The simplest way to illustrate the problem is to say that while all moral standards are ordinances from God, not all ordinances from God are moral standards. Yet typically evangelical users of worldview implicitly reject the latter half of this phrase. For example, Colson and Pearcey, in *How Now Shall We Live?*, while not explicitly equating moral order and cosmic order, focus a considerable amount of their analysis on specifically moral areas, such as the right to life, respect for the disabled, sexuality, and family,[30] and they typically make statements such as the following rebuttal of naturalism: ". . . Christianity claims that God created the universe with a definite structure—a material order and a moral order."[31] Again, in their critique of contemporary art, Colson and Pearcey tend to focus on the examples that are most obviously morally questionable, such as Robert Mapplethorp.[32] Other examples of this often implicit conflation of morality and creation order are easy to find.[33]

What, then, is at stake if my assertion about the need for a distinction between moral order and cosmic order is correct? Although evangelicals are quite familiar with the language of morality, they often seem

30 Colson and Pearcey, *How Now Shall We Live?* Chaps. 11–14, 20–25, 33.

31 Colson and Pearcey, *How Now Shall We Live?* 310; cf. 148, 196. Even Naugle falls into this way of speaking on occasion. For example, he observes that "this divinely grounded *moral* architecture—external to all human thinking, believing, or acting—consists of a prescription of virtue for human character and a set of laws governing human conduct" (*Worldview*, 262, emphasis added).

32 Colson and Pearcey, *How Now Shall We Live?* 449ff. I want to be careful here, for it is fashionable in some quarters today to suggest that even the most specific moral standards found in Scripture are in some way historically relative. The most common form of this is to assert that in the Bible the one abiding standard is *love* or *mercy*, but the specific ways of loving God and neighbor vary. So, for example, the Biblical condemnation of unrepentant homosexual practice is really not true for us. One such example of this thinking by a scholar who is an expert in Dooyeweerd's thought is Hendrik Hart. See his article "How I Came to See Paul's References to Homosexuality in a Radically New Light," in *The Other Side* (July–August 1992), 57–62.

33 See, for example, the Worldview Academy materials cited earlier (*Student Notebook* 33–38), and Herbert Schlossberg and Marvin Olasky, *Turning Point: A Christian Worldview Declaration* (Wheaton: Crossway Books, 1987), in which much of their commentary is devoted to focusing on Christians opposing slavery, abortion, sexual perversion, and the denigration of the family. The problem is not with having these issues addressed but with calling such an address a "worldview declaration," as though these examples somehow exhaust all that about which a worldview should be concerned.

unaware of how problematic this language is outside of specifically moral aspects of life. For example, you could read a publication such as this one in which you might discover some well-written chapters and some not-so-well-written chapters. Presumably, the bad ones were less than glorifying of God. Are the writers responsible for these bad articles guilty of immorality? Likewise, there are the great songs of praise of the Christian church and there are praise-and-worship ditties. Are the faults of the latter a moral failing? As a rookie teacher, I once gave an ethics (!) test that was too long for the allotted test period. When the fifty minutes were up, even my best students had to turn in tests with questions unanswered. Was my mistake in writing this test the result of a lack of educational sense or a lack of morals?

You see my point. Evangelicals today are striving commendably to become agents of redemption in a sin-sick culture. That is good and Godly. But if evangelicals do this solely with the language of morality, we will not have advanced very far from what went on before worldview thinking—judging cultural affairs as though the *only* law of God that applied was the moral law.

You may ask "how is this connected to worldview?" In the context of the thinkers who introduced worldview to the evangelical world, Kuyper and Dooyeweerd, *worldview* was the name for the basic pretheoretical experience of the world rooted in the heart, and this experience involved an awareness of creation order. It was no accident that Dooyeweerd referred to his work as "cosmonomic."[34] The *cosmos* is law-ordered, *nomic*, and one's worldview inescapably recognizes (because the laws and norms were inescapably present in creation) the lawful character of creation and what is taken to be the source of law. But this pretheoretical awareness also involved an awareness of the relatively distinct aspects of creation, such as knowing that a badly designed test is not immoral.

In this sense, the concept of worldview, while having significant epistemological import, is equally significant *ontologically*.[35] Laws and norms

---

34   For a succinct discussion of how the *Wijsbegeerte der wetsidee* (literally, "philosophy of the law-idea") was translated into English as "philosophy of the cosmonomic idea," see L. Kalsbeek, *Contours of a Christian Philosophy: An Introduction to Herman Dooyeweerd's Thought* (Toronto: Wedge, 1975), Chap. 6. This volume remains the most thorough technical introduction to Dooyeweerd's philosophy in English, although Clouser's *Myth* is excellent and generally more accessible to English speakers today. Naugle also comments on the meaning of "cosmonomic" (*Worldview*, 265).

35   I would take issue with the view expressed by Sire in numerous places in *Naming the Elephant* (41–44, 55–56, 69–73, 88, 118) that Biblical worldview is primarily an ontological matter. I would affirm his desire to break out of the dead-end of the modern and postmodern obsession with epistemology and recover a biblically sound ontology, but

are *real* but not physical. This view was and is a critical realist position, as Naugle recognizes,[36] but not as "realist" as is used by many evangelicals. This is why reducing the creation order to real physical and real moral laws, as most evangelicals still do, is inadequate to the full-orbed meaning of worldviewish thinking. Implied within a full-orbed meaning of worldview is the idea that all of creation is ordered by God and that this order is real and really present in the creation. Since not all of creation, including human culture, can be understood in terms of moral order, treating morality as the only type of creation order will inevitably lead to a truncated view of what is ordered by God and what counts as culture.[37]

I hope that the increasing and fruitful use of worldview in evangelical thought will continue. But I fear that unless the issues I have raised are at least acknowledged, if not addressed, the "worldview" tree will cease to bear fruit and evangelicals will wonder (again) why their attempts at a bigger notion of the Kingdom of God ended up so small.

---

this "either it's epistemology or it's ontology" dilemma is false. As the best of twentieth-century phenomenology and existentialism has shown, the two cannot be separated, a view which I would assert to be biblical.

36   Naugle, *Worldview*, 324ff.

37   Another area where I think evangelical users of "worldview" often get themselves into trouble is their tendency to uncritically appropriate the traditional notion of *analogia entis*. The question of the continuity of created being with the "being" of God is a crucial one, and it is my contention that, unlike many evangelicals, the Christian originators of the concept of worldview emphasized the transcendence of God and the radical mysteriousness of how God could still be active in the creation.

Worldview: An Untimely Meditation

Aron Reppmann

In this essay, I address the question: Does promoting a Christian worldview fulfill the mandate of Christian higher education? My answer to this question is both "yes" and "no." Specifically, I contend that there are elements in the concept of Christian worldview that have been fruitful for equipping ourselves and our students to engage our time and culture in prophetically responsive ways. I also contend, however, that some of the most important features of the concept of Christian worldview have not been fully recognized or faithfully developed in our handling of it. I propose that the full potential of "Christian worldview" for Christian higher education will be realized only if our accustomed ways of presenting Christian worldview are expanded in ways that some of the most influential proponents of the language and conceptuality of Christian worldview have been markedly hesitant about.

I develop this account in two sections. In the first section, I examine two features of the concept of Christian worldview that have been particularly fruitful over that concept's history, due to their appropriateness to the circumstances and needs of the time. In the second section, I argue that these two features, in spite of their fruitfulness so far, have not been fully developed or consistently adhered to. Along with this critical account, I include some practical proposals for remedying these failures in ways that will help the concept of worldview to further support the task of Christian higher education in our own time.

I.   Just in time: Some elements of the concept worldview that have been well suited to the needs of the day

1.   *Cultural opportunism*
A number of writers have observed that when the language of Christian worldview was initially introduced in the late nineteenth century by such thinkers as Abraham Kuyper and James Orr, there was a canny, strategic character to their choice of terms and concepts. The idea of

worldview itself was all the rage in the European intellectual climate of their time; the worldview concept was a slick German export that was well engineered to fit the needs of an age that was caught, as Gregory Clark writes, "between empirical skepticism and dogmatic rationalism."[1] David Naugle writes:

> The radical shift in the metaphysical underpinnings of the West called for a new strategy, and the fashionable German conception of *Weltanschauung* provided the key. . . . To satisfy the need for an understanding of human existence, Dilthey proposes his doctrine of worldviews in which he attempts to steer a middle course between a defunct metaphysical absolutism and the nihilism of historical relativism.[2]

This well-targeted concept found a ready reception; "by the 1840's," writes Albert Wolters, the word *Weltanschauung* "had become a standard item in the vocabulary of the educated German, denoting a global outlook on life and the world—akin to philosophy but without its rational pretensions."[3] By using the then intellectually fashionable language of worldview to describe the Christian experience, Kuyper, Orr, and others sought to provide a timely, strategic point of contact between Christians and the leading intellectual and cultural currents of their day.

In adopting the language of worldview as a description for their Christian stance, thinkers such as Kuyper and Orr engaged their surrounding culture by accepting, even eagerly welcoming, the currency of their time; the worldview concept was "timely" in the sense that it was fashionable. To borrow a term from a later generation, worldview was "hip," and the pioneers of Christian worldview thinking exploited this widespread popularity to demonstrate the continuing relevance of their anciently grounded Christian form of life.

There was also, however, another kind of timeliness at work in the development of the strategic discourse of Christian worldview, the kind of timeliness that is practiced not simply by speaking in the familiar and popular language of the people of one's own time, but by pointedly using that language to say things that those people are not particularly predisposed to hear but desperately need. This prophetic way of speaking seems "untimely" insofar as it questions and challenges the cherished assumptions of one's time, but actually it is very timely in its urgent appeal to the needs of the time.[4] In this way, too, the language of Christian worldview,

---

1   Clark, "The Nature of Conversion," 207.
2   Naugle, *Worldview*, 8, 85.
3   Wolters, "On the Idea of Worldview and Its Relation to Philosophy," 15.
4   Among modern philosophers, one striking practitioner of this prophetic way of speak-

as it found its way into intellectual and especially academic life, has provided a particularly timely strategy for Christian cultural engagement. I explore this strategy in the following section.

2. *Emphasis on the crucial role of pretheoretical commitments in human life*

Basic to the idea of worldview, as it was first formulated within the cultural universe of German Idealism and Romanticism, is that human beings are, to a great extent, determined by the particular way of life in which they find themselves, the specific location whose address is made up of the "cult, code, and creed" of the community to which they belong, whose story they cannot help but participate in, a story that is even built into the structures and patterns of the community's language and other social practices. The concept of worldview calls attention to the ways in which we are rooted in the cultural soil that nourishes us. Although our view of the world is not simply limited to that specific location, it always starts from such specificity, from the particularity of a perspective. Like trees, our capability for rising above the limitations of our particular starting point is always conditioned, supported, and, yes, particularized and limited by that starting point. We can no more bootstrap ourselves entirely out of the thick, rich, life-sustaining cultural muck in which we find ourselves than a tree can uproot itself out of its own soil.[5]

Those who initially adopted the language and conceptuality of worldview as a way of articulating the way of life of the Christian community emphasized in particular the rootedness of worldview in the pretheoretical soil of faith, the basic and ultimate trust that precedes and grounds all attempts to articulate it or anything else. James Olthuis clearly represents a continuation of this emphasis in our own day when he describes worldview as

---

ing to one's contemporaries—seemingly out of step with the times, but fact keenly oriented to them—is Friedrich Nietzsche. One of his descriptions of this practice, a description I have borrowed in the title of this paper, is the phrase *unzeitgemäße Betrachtungen*, which can be translated as "untimely meditations." See, for example, the most well-known of his four *Unzeitgemäße Betrachtungen, Vom Nutzen und Nachteil der Historie für das Leben* (1873), translated by Peter Preuss as *On the Advantage and Disadvantage of History for Life* (Indianapolis: Hackett, 1980).

5   Although the formulators of German Idealism and Romanticism especially emphasized the particularity of all human perspectives and the concomitant inability to absolutely transcend one's culturally located starting point, they were not the first philosophers to call attention to this situation and to shape their philosophies in light of it. For instance, Drew Hyland, in his book *Finitude and Transcendence in the Platonic Dialogues* (SUNY: 1995), argues that these emphases pervade the writings of the ancient philosopher Plato.

. . . a medium of mediation and integration in a two-way movement between the commitment of faith and all other modes of human experience. Certainty received in the surrender of faith leads via the mediation of a worldview to a way of living. Concomitantly, a way of life, in all its modes and moments, influences via a worldview the commitment of faith.[6]

In this formulation of the worldview concept, faith is not simply one element of historical particularity among all of the others that determine our particular cultural location. Rather, faith is acknowledged as the crucial factor that orients how anyone encounters, negotiates, and integrates the other elements of her particular cultural matrix; while those other elements also have an effect on the particular shape of one's faith, no other element is singled out as so crucially determinative. Noting this emphasis as a common tendency among a number of contemporary advocates of Christian worldview thinking, the editors of *Stained Glass* write of "a specifically Christian understanding of the 'rootedness' of worldviews in religious commitment" as the standard by which Christian applications of the worldview concept must be measured.[7]

While this emphasis on the crucial and often determinative role of pretheoretical, religious trust was consistent with the broadly popular and widely disseminated cultural language of worldview that I described earlier, things became more complicated and contentious when Christian worldview thinkers brought this emphasis purposely into the academy. Particularly under the leadership of Abraham Kuyper, with his ambitions for the culturally formative and philosophically robust role of worldview-conscious, faith-filled thinking in his Free University, this movement's commitment to foregrounding the living relationship between ultimate trust and articulated worldview was no longer safely kept out of the intellectual "high culture" of the academy. Wolters writes of the contrast between traditional western (or, I would say, at least modern) philosophy's "emphasis on the universal, abstract, eternal, and identical character" of our viewing and worldview thinking's "emphasis on the particular, concrete, temporal, and unique character of that viewing."[8] To Wolters' catalogue of philosophy's traditional emphases, I would add the exclusivistic and individualistic intellectualism of philosophizing as it has been practiced in the context of the modern university.

When worldview thinking was introduced into the academy itself

---

6   James Olthuis, "On Worldviews," 28.
7   Marshall, Griffioen, and Mouw, *Stained Glass*, 11.
8   Wolters, "On the Idea of Worldview and Its Relation to Philosophy," 18.

as a purposeful strategy for a committed community of faith to bring its cultural and intellectual program to scholarly expression,[9] this contrast became a confrontation, profoundly affecting the ways in which scholars (at the Free University as well as at many other institutions that have followed its lead in this regard) addressed themselves to their own work, to the heritage of the western philosophical tradition, and to their philosophical colleagues anywhere else they could get a hearing. By emphasizing the crucial role of pretheoretical commitments, and particularly that of faith, this articulation of Christian worldview thinking has provided a healthy critique of the exclusivistic, individualistic, overly rationalized philosophical industry, cut off from the living concerns of wisdom, that has dominated much of the elite intellectual world of western universities.[10]

These, then, are two ways in which the concept of Christian worldview has been remarkably appropriate to the time in which it was introduced and to much of the time since. But where are we now? Do we find ourselves "after" worldview? And what are we "after" in our own practice of Christian higher education framed by worldview talk? In the second part of this paper, I return to the two elements of Christian worldview thinking that I have just described, to point out some ways in which they have not been developed as fully as they might be, a failure that I believe is a leading cause of the current uncertainty about whether worldview fulfills the mandate of Christian liberal-arts education.

II.   "For such a time as this?"

Many theorists of Christian worldview, even those who practiced the timely strategies I have described, have been notably insecure about the historical particularity of the worldview-concept—or perhaps sometimes negligent of that particularity.[11] This insecurity about the particular historical location of the concept of worldview plays itself out with regard

---

9   "Scholarly expression" is my translation of the phrase *wetenschappelijke uitdrukking,* which Valentinus Hepp, writing in 1923, used to describe the relationship of an "independent Christian philosophy" (for whose development he was appealing) to "the [existing] Reformed world and life view" (quoted at Wolters, "On the Idea of Worldview and Its Relation to Philosophy," 21).

10   Calvin Seerveld dedicates his contribution to this collection in loving memory of Pete Steen; although I did not know Steen personally, I take what I am describing here to have been his particular calling of scholarly service in this world—to take the scandalous confrontation of worldview-conscious, serious philosophizing anywhere and everywhere he could find a hearing for it.

11   With the appearance of David Naugle's *Worldview: The History of a Concept* and its growing prominence in discussions of Christian worldview, the negligent no longer have any excuse!

to both of the strategies I have indicated. I come back to both of them, in reverse order, and include in my discussion some practical proposals for addressing this situation.

1. *Fear of the pretheoretical—particularly the historical*

Although the worldview concept's emphasis on the crucial role of the pretheoretical, specifically applied to the role of faith, has been welcome among proponents of Christian worldview thinking, those same proponents have been notably hesitant about acknowledging another significant pretheoretical feature in the concept of worldview, namely its cultural and historical particularity.[12]   On one hand, we frequently find this concept treated as though it were a once-for-all or even timeless truth. In this tendency, all of the diversity of Christian ways of encountering and viewing the world is reduced to this one articulation, which is particularly modern (drawing as it does on a conceptuality developed in response to identifiably modern philosophical and cultural problematics). Furthermore, this approach of ignoring the particular and not specifically Christian cultural soil out of which the worldview concept grew leads to treating Christianity's relationship to the wider sphere of human cultural endeavor strictly in antagonistic, oppositional terms, as an absolute struggle in which "the" Christian worldview must prove its value by demonstrating its comprehensive triumph over any and every other system of cultural meaning.[13]

On the other hand, some of those who use the language of Christian worldview and are aware of the particular cultural history of the worldview concept have been noticeably uncomfortable with this particularity, insecure about whether the specific cultural and historical location of worldview language make it unsuitable as a vehicle for expressing the stance of Christians in the world. They ask, is this concept safe, or is it irreparably tainted by its association with the historical particularities of post-Kantian philosophizing? In this way, these thinkers worry that the

---

12   This represents yet another way in which worldview is "untimely" (see footnote 4 above).

13   This reduction of all of Christian thought and experience to a single articulated worldview, and the accompanying antagonistic and triumphalistic stance toward all other human cultural endeavor, is evident throughout Charles Colson's and Nancy Pearcey's influential treatment of Christian worldview thinking, *How Now Shall We Live?* The book jacket provides an apt summary of this approach: "Colson and Pearcey show that all other worldviews fail to meet the test of rational consistency or practical application in the real world. Only the Christian worldview provides a rationally sustainable way to understand the universe. Only the Christian worldview fits the real world and can be lived out consistently in every area of life."

particular cultural and historical situatedness of the worldview concept make it either outdated and passé or heretically compromised.[14]

However, the historical particularity of the worldview concept, its point of origin in a specific time and place in human culture, should not be a reason for anxiety or avoidance. Rather, acknowledging this historical location is analogous to the already well-established admission that our engagement with reality is rooted in the pretheoretical, prereflective soil of faith as ultimate trust. As we have seen, Christian worldview thinkers are very familiar with the latter admission, many of them even insisting on it as a requirement for conceiving of worldview in a distinctly Christian way. By understanding faith as basic trust, proponents of Christian worldview have affirmed that, while we may give an account of faith, that account will never be fully rationalized; if faith is "properly basic," there remains something about it that is, from our human standpoint, contingent and unexplained, something for which we can be profoundly grateful and which we can endeavor to understand but the limits of which we will not fully transcend, since we are finite human creatures. Cultural and historical locatedness is a similarly pervasive element of our creaturely human finitude. Finding yourself always already enmeshed in a story, which you have not begun and which you will not see through to its close, is a profound element of pretheoretical life and is built into the fabric of what it means to be a finite creature of God. As human creatures, we are called to responsibility, to respond to our finite creaturely situation not by gaining some kind of absolute transcendence of historical human culture but by being gratefully faithful to the circumstances in which we find ourselves.

In light of this awareness of historicity (including the historicity of our concepts) as a legitimate element of finite, creaturely human life, I suggest that we can improve our handling of the worldview concept's his-

---

14   In this vein, Wolters writes: "The notion of worldview has intimate historical and systematic connections with modern humanistic views of history, science, and religion; it is, in fact, virtually defined by those views. This leaves us with a crucial question: Can Christians who are fundamentally critical of the spirit of modernity—particularly as it manifests itself in historicism, the autonomy of science, and the privatization of religion—salvage the idea of *Weltanschauung* and use it for our own systematic purposes?" ("On the Idea of Worldview and Its Relation to Philosophy," 19). In a similar way, William Rowe uses images associated with maintaining "homeland security": "The concept of worldview is not a native but rather an immigrant into Christian intellectual territory. And, like all immigrants, it has crossed our borders with its baggage in hand. It is possible . . . to conduct a kind of border search, opening the linguistic suitcases of the worldview idea in order to examine the contents for semantic contraband" (Rowe, "Society After the Subject, Philosophy After the Worldview," 156).

torical particularity in two ways. The first has to do with how we handle the origins of the concept of worldview. When we make use of this concept to articulate the meaningfulness of Christian living in the world, whether we do this with and for our students or in our engagement of the broader scholarly world, we can do so in a way that neither ignores nor fears the particular rooting of this concept in specific historical developments of modern intellectual life. Rather, we can deliberately thematize this history, calling it to attention as something interesting and as an earlier part of a story in which we ourselves participate.[15]

My second suggestion has to do with how we handle the ongoing history of the worldview concept, down to and including our own time. We can attend in a self-conscious way to the particular role that worldview talk has played in our particular communities, disciplinary contexts, institutional and confessional contexts, and so on. In a way, this means perpetually asking the question, "what it is that we are after when we pursue worldview?" since the answer to that question is bound to keep changing somewhat in different situations.[16] For instance, in my own institution, Trinity Christian College, the institutional role of worldview talk has shifted somewhat over time. In the 1950's and early 1960's, the general intellectual context in North America was one in which "objectivity" was honored and religious commitments were suspect. A general assumption was that the operational standards of the exact sciences provided the most appropriate guidelines for all academic endeavor. In response to that situation, an emphasis on worldview was a way of staking out a strong, principled, and liberating resistance to the dominant intellectual ethos. Later, with the great social and intellectual upheavals of the late 1960's and early 1970's, an attentiveness to worldview provided a strong point of connection to (but also critique of) newer intellectual movements that emphasized the ways in which such pre-theoretical features as ideology, social class, gender, and ethnicity shape academic theorizing. More recently, as Trinity's population of faculty and students has become more confessionally and ethnically diverse, worldview has be-

---

15   David Naugle's *Worldview: The History of a Concept* provides a very valuable resource for such thematization, although it seems to me that in his "concluding reflections" on the "benefits" and "dangers" of worldview, he shies away somewhat from accepting the effects of historicity in the way that I am arguing for (Naugle, *Worldview*, 331–45).

16   For a similar argument about another matter of Christian cultural concern, see Richard Mouw's emphasis on the need to understand the different cultural context of common-grace theology today as compared to earlier articulations: Richard Mouw, *He Shines in All That's Fair: Culture and Common Grace.* Grand Rapids: Eerdmans, 2002), 12–13.

come important as a new marker of our shared identity and purpose: in spite of our ethnic and confessional differences, an appeal to the need to discover and foster a biblically rooted Christian worldview can unite us by offering us a shared vision of what identifies us as a community. Used in these historically sensitive and probing ways, the idea of worldview would provide us more with a way of framing our questions than with a pre-packaged set of answers; it would be a place to stand and survey the cultural work to be done, not a patio or a rocking-chair on which to sit.[17]

2. *Neglecting the "cultural opportunism" of the worldview concept*

Whenever we ignore or diminish the story of this concept's emergence, whether by absolutizing the idea of worldview or by suggesting that it is too intimately linked to the cultural circumstances in which it emerged, we dishonor the faith-filled ingenuity of our culturally opportunistic Christian-worldview predecessors. Aside from the basic viciousness of such dishonor, this move has the effect of cutting us off from the need and the opportunity to think in an analogous way about our own time. When the concept of Christian worldview becomes too fixed and settled in our institutions, an account without a story—that is, when it becomes an ideology—we let ourselves off the hook of having to ask ourselves what cultural strategies would be as appropriate for our time as the concept of Christian worldview was for the turn of the last century.

For us to engage in a similarly timely cultural opportunism, two things are necessary. The first is the attention to the historic origins and ongoing development of the concept of worldview that I have already urged; by requiring ourselves and our students to read closely the history of the emergence (or the construction) of the idea of Christian worldview, we will be better equipped to imitate them in our somewhat different circumstances.[18]

The second necessary thing is for us to be attentive to precisely those

---

17   On Christian worldview as "a way of framing the question" rather than "a recipe for finding answers," see Wolters, *Creation Regained: Biblical Basics for a Reformational Worldview*, 2nd ed. (Grand Rapids: Eerdmans, 2005), 96–98.

18   On worldview as ideology, the remarks of Brian Walsh and Sylvia Keesmaat are striking: "Singular views of the world come at a price. To maintain their own singular superiority, they must negate all other visions, all other narratives. That is to say, worldviews have a tendency to become absolutistic ideologies which forget that they are particular ways of conceiving life that have been constituted by particular traditions, religions or communities in particular times and places. Worldviews-turned-ideologies present their view of the world as simply the way the world is. They are world*views* that function so well that it is forgotten that they are 'views'" (Brian Walsh and Sylvia Keesmaat. *Colossians Remixed: Subverting the Empire*. Downers Grove: InterVarsity, 2004. 99).

"somewhat different circumstances," to participate in the current cultural discussion with an imaginative eye out for discourses and cultural strategies that we could appropriate in a way that is timely—both in the ordinary sense of speaking the language of our time and in the prophetic sense of challenging the assumptions of our time. On the face of it, this strategic participation seems to be a more difficult task today than it was in the world of late-nineteenth-century high European culture. Higher education and culturally influential discourse have become much more widely diffused in the intervening time, so that they are no longer as overwhelmingly the possession of a group of people relatively unified by gender, ethnicity, and social class. Although this is in many ways a very good thing, it does mean that it is more difficult today to identify a shared terminology or cultural outlook that tends to unite highly educated people; every candidate for such a discourse or perspective risks being discredited by one or another group as driven by an ideological or political agenda.

Nevertheless, in spite of this difficulty, there are several recent, noteworthy efforts to participate in a timely and strategic way in the significant cultural discussions of our time, taking as their points of engagement such concerns as environmentalism, empire, and globalization.[19] In these various efforts, we see Christian scholars working to engage our time in a way that speaks its most treasured languages while at the same time infiltrating the strongholds of its ideologies. I trust that these and similar efforts will bring new fruit, even though it will be unsettling and challenging for those of us (myself included) who have become comfortable with a particular, sedimented articulation of the shape and purpose of a Christian worldview.

---

19   On environmentalism, see Steven Bouma-Prediger, *For the Beauty of the Earth* (Grand Rapids: Baker Academic, 2001). On empire, see Brian Walsh and Sylvia Keesmaat, *Colossians Remixed*. On globalization, see Lamin Sanneh and Joel Carpenter, ed., *The Changing Face of Christianity* (Oxford University Press, 2005). One marker of the continuing fruitfulness of the idea of worldview is that these new efforts frequently integrate insights from the language of worldview, even as they implicitly or explicitly challenge the hegemony of the worldview concept over Christian engagement with culture; see, for example, Bouma-Prediger on the "worldview crisis" occasioned by environmental disaster (*For the Beauty of the Earth*, 85).

Works Cited

Bouma-Prediger, Steven. *For the Beauty of the Earth: A Christian Vision for Creation Care.* Grand Rapids: Baker Academic, 2001.

Clark, Gregory. "The Nature of Conversion: How the Rhetoric of World-view Philosophy Can Betray Evangelicals." In *The Nature of Confession: Evangelicals and Postliberals in Conversation*, edited by Timothy R. Phillips and Dennis L. Okholm, 201–18. Downers Grove: InterVarsity, 1996.

Colson, Charles, and Nancy Pearcey. *How Now Shall We Live?* Wheaton: Tyndale House, 1999.

Hyland, Drew. *Finitude and Transcendence in the Platonic Dialogues.* Albany: SUNY, 1995.

Marshall, Paul A., Sander Griffioen, and Richard J. Mouw, ed. *Stained Glass: Worldviews and Social Science.* Lanham: University Press of America, 1989.

Mouw, Richard. *He Shines in All That's Fair: Culture and Common Grace.* Grand Rapids: Eerdmans, 2002.

Naugle, David. *Worldview: The History of a Concept.* Grand Rapids: Eerdmans, 2002.

Nietzsche, Friedrich. *The Advantage and Disadvantage of History for Life*, translated by Peter Preuss (1873). Indianapolis and Cambridge: Hackett, 1980.

Olthuis, James. "On Worldviews." In Marshall, et al., *Stained Glass*, 26–40.

Rowe, William V. "Society After the Subject, Philosophy After the Worldview." In Marshall, et al., *Stained Glass*, 156–83.

Sanneh, Lamin, and Joel Carpenter. *The Changing Face of Christianity: Africa, the West, and the World.* Oxford and New York: Oxford University Press, 2005.

Walsh, Brian, and Sylvia Keesmaat. *Colossians Remixed: Subverting the Empire.* Downers Grove: InterVarsity, 2004.

Wolters, Albert M. *Creation Regained: Biblical Basics for a Reformational Worldview.* 2nd ed. Grand Rapids: Eerdmans, 2005.

———. "On the Idea of Worldview and Its Relation to Philosophy." In Marshall, et al., *Stained Glass*, 14–25.

The Damages of a Christian Worldview[1]

CALVIN SEERVELD

Now large crowds of people were fellow-traveling with Jesus. Turning to them, Jesus said:

"If anyone comes to follow me but is more attached to father and mother, spouse and children, brothers and sisters, yes, is more committed to one's own life than to me, that person cannot be one of my disciples. Whoever does not carry his or her own cross in coming to follow my [Way] cannot be my disciple.

"For who of you willing to build a tower does not first sit down to count up the cost, to check out whether you have (enough) to bring it to completion? Otherwise, when you have laid a foundation and are not able to bring the building to completion, all those watching will begin to ridicule you saying, 'This fellow began to build but was not able to bring it off!'

"Or, what ruler going to encounter another ruler in war will not first sit down and deliberate whether one is able with 10,000 to meet up with the other coming toward him with 20,000? And if not, while the other is still a good distance off, asks, by sending off a delegation, what will it take for peace?

"Somewhat like that then: all of you who do not say goodbye to all that you yourself own, cannot be my disciple.

"Sure, salt is good. But if the salt becomes saltless, in what way will you be able to make it salty (again)? It is not fit for the earth nor for the manure pile—they throw it out.

"Whoever has ears to hear, let that man or woman hear."

(Luke 14:25-35)

In preparing to come to this conference, as I reviewed some of the literature on "worldview" and "Christian worldview" published in the last twenty years—the essays in *Stained Glass* (edited by Paul Marshall, Sander Griffioen, and Richard Mouw, 1989), the solid book by David Naugle (Eerdmans, 2002) and publications he refers to in his Appendix A, plus various other readings—I thought, what an embarrassment of riches! You could get the impression that among evangelical Christians it

---

1   In loving memory of Pete Steen (1936–1984).

is almost fashionable to have or consider having "a Christian worldview" as a tower of defensive strength to do battle with the "postmodern" enemy armies at the gates.

I wondered if, in the spirit of the theme of this conference as I understand it, "After Worldview," I could complicate matters a bit, join in the conversation, and suggest why the Christ's encouragement and warning to his fellow-travelers in Luke 14 might be an appropriate Word of the Lord to remember at this juncture. Have we who have been building a Christian worldview counted the costs of bringing a Christian world-and-life vision to completion as we introduce its contours to a public and rising college generation? The cost of genuine discipleship in following the Rule of Jesus Christ is quite stiff if it is not wholehearted, does not stay salty, or defaults on follow-through. What are the damages of a Christian worldview?

Defining "Worldview" as a "World-and-Life Vision" Distinct from a "Way of Life"

Let me begin *in media res* with the working definition I should like to be responsible for: a worldview is a conscious, quasi-synoptic world-and-life vision of everything all together, which is imaginative and literarily suggestive in quality rather than theoretically precise, which structures and can guide one's concrete experience in God's ordered cosmos.[2]

This terminology helps me clarify, I think, various matters found in the literature and lets me note: *not everybody has a world-and-life vision.* Every sane human being, whether aware of it or not, does have, in my judgment, a "way of life," a subconscious habit of activity that is not a studied reflective view but is a pattern that hangs together and gets beaten out in the press of daily life. A person is inducted into a way of life at birth along with one's mother tongue. Sometimes called "ethic," this *habitus* one unthinkingly inhabits is an historically worked-in formation corporately held, a tradition of wonts shaped by underlying faith commitment, passed on by common consent, certified by specific rites and rituals, which notably shows its assumed cohesive grip on one's life in crises.

In the provincial rural New York community where I grew up, sons routinely followed in the occupation of their father, married early, raised a family, became prosperous, and grew older, and their sons followed the same cycle. In pre so-called World War II–Italy, a similar way of life

---

2   Paraphrasing a section of C. Seerveld, *Skeleton to Philosophy* (Chicago: Trinity Christian College mimeographed typescript, 1960).

would be followed, except the eldest son would be offered to the priest-hood.

Once upon a time there was a Western Humanist way of life called civility, where without question when the Titanic was sinking, children and women went first into the lifeboats.

If your way of life happened to be a walk with the Lord informed by the preached Scripture like Micah 6:6–8, Matthew 5–7, and Romans 13:8–10, when the Dutch teacher H. de Jongste (who translated the bulk of Herman Dooyeweerd's *A New Critique of Theoretical Thought*, 1953–1958) answered the knock on his door one night during German troop occupation in the 1940s and faced two downed American airmen, what do you instinctively do, knowing that if the Nazi informer who lives above you finds out, it could mean the death of you and your family? Of course, you take them in and hide them.

For me, a person's way of life is inescapably basic, the primary out-working of one's entrusting faith orientation in God's world, whatever the faith be. A way of life is the contour of what one tacitly takes for granted as meaningful. Sander Griffioen calls my subconscious way of life a *Weltbild*: "the common outlook of a people, society, or culture; it is apprehended and appropriated in an unconscious manner; it is rela-tively constant in time" (Griffioen 1989, 2). No wonder the persecutor Saul went looking for those "who belonged to *the Way*" (*hodos*), it says in Acts 9:2. The early Christians were not killed for their "views," but for their converted way of life described in Acts 2–8. And it is precisely because the apostate way of life inculcated subliminally in many postlit-erate American adults by the ubiquitous powerful pop-culture media and targeted advertising gets jolted into reflective consciousness by the cul-ture critique of a Christian world-and-life vision that makes a conscious Christian world-and-life vision a valuable aid in redemptive education.

When one's subconscious way of life reaches sustained consciousness, when a life pattern becomes roughly understood as a pattern of sorts, gets expressed, articulated with connections and ramifications, then you have the network, in my book, of a *Weltanschauung*, a world-and-life vision.

An indigenous tribal people can carry on living under its myths, but it takes a mythographer or a storyteller like Homer to weave a world of rudimentary powers (cf. Galatians 4:3, Colossians 2:8!) into a roster of superhuman gods and heroic demigod-like men to form a mythology that hangs together but still is not always systematically clear.

The Puritan world-and-life vision crystallized in John Bunyan's (1628–1688) robust tale of Pilgrim Christian's progress on the narrow road toward the Celestial City, with so many worldly sideshow attractions off limits, marshals together the tempting pitfalls and little accomplishments and blessings of a sober, persevering human life of faith with sure otherworldly horizons.

Gustav Mahler's (1860–1911) *Die Kindertotenlieder* (1901–1904, sung by Janet Baker or Shelley de Young) presents Friedrich Rückert's (1788–1866) Biedermeierish verse of Stoic grief transformed into a massive, poignant German Romanticist mesh of sound that encompasses human life and death with poignant Nietzschean *Weltschmerz*:

> Ein Lämplein verlosch in meinen Zelt!
> Heil! Heil sei dem Freudenlicht der Welt!

It would be wise, it seems to me, not to shrink the "world-and-life vision" designation down to a technical term "worldview," since it is the *pulse of life lived* that invigorates the imaginative narrative of a world-and-life vision. Fortunately, Abraham Kuyper (1837–1920) salvaged in his first Princeton Stone lecture (1898) from his intended *levens- en wereld-beschouwing* (life-and-world view) terminology, the emphasis on *life*, because he was concerned to counteract the accusation that Calvinism is only a narrow-minded dogmatics: "I desire to speak to you on Calvinism as an independent general tendency, which from a mother-principle of its own, has developed an independent form both for our *life* and for our *thought* among the nations of Western Europe and North America" (Kuyper's emphasis, 15). But Kuyper was ill-advised to call this principled world-encompassing consciousness "to furnish human society with a different method of existence, and to populate the world of the human heart with different ideals and conceptions" (17) a "life *system*" (11 n.1), because *system* overstates the conceptual form of a Calvinian world-and-life *vision*.

To approach an interrelating world-and-life vision, whether it be a Calvinian, Marxian, Muslim, or American Horatio Alger–Walt Disneyean vision of world and life, from the side of its bringing to self-consciousness a way of life in the world—weighting structural features like order and change, what is good and what is evil, setting up choices of priorities, deciding what is worth dying for—highlights better the sterling integrity and service of a world-and-life vision than coming at it from the German Idealist perspective of a *Weltanschauung*'s being a pretheoretical, somehow supraindividual contemplative "view" of the world. Maybe we do not have to worry about getting a baptismal certificate for "worldview" (Naugle, 289–90; Rowe, 156) if we conceive a "world-and-life vision" in terms of its being grounded in the biblical hint on *hodos*, that a world-and-life vision is born out of a cohering way of life sprung from one's faith.

A world-and-life vision is a comprehensive world map and a draught for action (Griffioen 2002, 287) to which one may be *committed*. J. P. A. Mekkes shunned the standard phrase and deliberately used the term *levensovertuiging*, life conviction, life persuasion (Klapwijk 1989, 43). I myself prefer to speak of a "*committed* world-and-life vision," to catch its far-reaching scope and its claim on one's heart—a feature Dilthey half-sensed in talking about *Streit der Weltanschauung*en. Now, I should like to introduce carefully a different uncanny dimension of creatural reality that intersects, I believe, the committed world-and-life visions (as well as ways of life) operative in many of us people.

If a committed world-and-life vision is an imaginative typical orientation that can be taken toward the *structural* features of our life world (what is there? how? why?), there is also the matter of *directional* choice on where are we headed? what Spirit drives you on in your world-and-life vision?

While World-and-Life Visions Get at Cosmic Structure, Direction Is a Matter of Being Spirit-led

There are biblical givens on how humans who, at heart, have been enlivened by the Holy Spirit and have become new(!) creatures (2 Corinthians 5:17, Ephesians 3:16–19) still struggle with the manifold power of *Sarx*, sin, in their bodily members (Romans 7:5–8:11, Ephesians 4:17–5:21). Holy Scripture makes clear that the resurrected Christ has indeed overcome the evil principalities and powers of this world (Ephesians 1:19–23, Colossians 1:15–23, 2:8–15), but all of us creatures alive must still contend with their demonic brutality (Ephesians 6:12). Evil spirits, often masquerading as angels of light (2 Corinthians 11:12–15), crave to reside in bodies, especially important bodies, officials, institutions, corporations, and only if necessary in a herd of swine (Mark 5:1–20). That's why Scripture says we must test the spirit of what is afoot and prophesied in society to know whether it be of God or the Lie (1 John 4:1–6).

I have been at important gatherings, I dare say, when you'd swear you could detect the acrid trace of a smell from some lower echelon devil lurking nearby in the room ready to befoul and derail the deliberations.

And I remember vividly a Friday afternoon meeting of Seventh Day Adventist leaders in Collonges-sous-Salève, France, I was invited to join (1989) where there had been hefty debates, but during the concluding communal prayers held as the sun quietly began to set and the Sabbath of rest began, you could sense a sweet communion settling like an angel down upon the group with a holy peace. Maybe that is why Karl Barth muses about angels as personal Power Point presentations/messengers of God's omnipotent will (*Die Kirchliche Dogmatik* III/3 par. 51).

When my wife and I attended a Black Panther rally in Chicago in the late 1960s, just to see what was going on, there was an altogether different spirit present than there had been in an assembly to hear Martin Luther King speak on nonviolent protest a year before. (There was no entrance fee to the Panther Rally, but you had to pay *to get out* of the meeting, a contribution to the Huey Newton Defense Fund.)

Before you think I am off track, let me quote you Walter Wink: "It is a virtue to disbelieve what does not exist. It is dangerous to disbelieve what exists outside our current limited categories" (Wink 1984, 4). Principalities and powers do exist, according to Scripture, and deeply affect our lives in the world.

"School spirit" is a much more fundamental matter than accrediting agencies may think, and it is the school principal or college president who usually functions as the lightning rod for the spirit of an institutional faculty and student body. One could also say that exorcism of written texts, images, and prophetic appeals called philosophy is at the crux of Christian education: teachers need to detect, expose, and cast out the evil spirit weaseling in the materials we deal with in classroom and lab. But then do not do exorcisms the way Pharisees do it, said Jesus, for show, with acclaim, triumphantly (Luke 11:14–23, 18:9–14, Matthew 23:1–12, Mark 9:38–41; cf. Acts 19:11–20). Scripture adjures us to reclaim those flesh-and-blood humans and their deeds, which are possessed by evil principalities and powers, and to do it by painstaking, prayerful probing that leads to the truth by doing justice to the writings and forging peace because one's own imaginative competence and humbled analysis—God help us—is led by "the sword of the Holy Spirit, which is the Word of God" (Ephesians 6:10–20).

If we keep this matter of *spirited direction* in humans (following God's holy will though plagued by disobedience *versus* godless enslavement to evil principalities though kept human by God's grace), keep the matter of *spirited direction* distinct from our human overall vision of the structural constancies and changes in God's world, it puts a more complicated spin on the nature and relative salience of our committed world-and-life visions, which are also always Spirit-driven.

Let me draw out just three implications for discussion purposes.

1. *World-and-life visions are not incommensurable*
   and can provide knowledge to the wise

There are different world-and-life visions to which people are committed because different basic positions can be taken on various realities
of world and life that impinge willy-nilly on our consciousness; namely,
is everything a *uni*verse? what is the makeup of the world and the relative
place of human life? where does the buck stop? and are there criteria for
meaning?

One popular world-and-life vision throughout the ages has been the
vision that change is constant and reality is an evolutionary (or devolu-
tionary) process in which the fittest survive. That world-and-life vision
shaped ancient Chalcedonian Thrasymachus's stance on political justice
(might makes right), Renaissance Pico della Mirandola's (1463–1494)
take on the chameleon nature of man (we can become devils or angels),
and guided Milton Friedman's (1912–2006) unlimited free market money policy for the nation. *Good for the best!*

A quite different world-and-life vision imagines that sameness is
heaven, absolute unchanging law and paradigmatic order is what counts
as real; neglect what seems bad, troubles are illusionary. Such a stationary
world-and-life vision has permeated the contemplative quietism of Zen
Buddhism from time immemorial: endure the *fata morgana samsura* and
await to be transfixed by the state of *nirvana*. The so-called International
Style of architecture, a weakened derivative of Mies van der Rohe's genius (1886–1969), has carried a rationalized version of Mondrianic bal-
anced stability and inhuman sameness throughout the whole world in its
standardized rectangular high-rise domiciles and office buildings. *Remain
unmoved!*

Another favorite world-and-life vision, considered to be as solid as
the Rock of Ages, is the one that only counts the birds in the hand: your
fitness health, your accumulated wealth, and a good conversation over
a martini at the tenth hole is what it is all about. Hellenistic hedonists,
even Borgia pope Alexander VI (1492–1503), and sybaritic yuppies today in both East and West all work out this simple world-and-life vision
with gusto. *Carpe diem!*

Or a world-and-life vision of quite a different tack has people mes-
merized by the occult, an invisible *mysterium tremendum*, what is alchem-
ically hidden in the numinous Dark Night of Universal Unconscious
Soul. This is the perennial world-and-life vision of Gnostics, Jewish Kab-
balists, the Masonic lodge of Tolstoi's day (1828–1910), TM, and those
who live by astrology and horoscopes. *Become initiate to the Secrets!*

But you know all of this. There are an indefinite number of world-and-life visions extant today, recurrent in history, available to format your consciousness because there are many ways to construe (misconstrue) the structural pressure points of the realties enveloping us. Each of these bona fide world-and-life visions are imaginatively consistent and hang together, depending on the tinted eyeglasses you accept to peruse life in God's world. "They are divergent, contrary, conflicting, but are not incommensurable" (Griffioen 1998, 125–26), because they are fabricated and held by nonstupid human persons dealing with the same reality, who grab hold of the elephant at a different place, and give priority to and valorize different structural features of world and life.

What I want to suggest is that opposing world-and-life visions are not mortal enemies for followers of Jesus Christ, but are just bad neighbors, *neighbors*. And a communion of Christians who consciously develop 20/20 biblical vision can *learn from* mistaken world-and-life visions even as we sinful saints examine such astigmatic visions and refocus what has been taken crookedly amiss, distorted, wrongly cleft, and reductionistically oversimplified.

Those who know that it is *not* "good for the best!" but have a vision of "blessed are the meek!" (Matthew 5:3–10) can still learn from Darwinian protagonists that "meek" does not mean "seek the martyrdom of being steamrollered." Christians who respond to God's injunction to become "mature" (*teleioi*, Matthew 5:48, Hebrews 5:14–6:3) rather than "stand pat unmoved," can still learn from the rock-ribbed who believe "the Western canon is the canon—that's it!" that "newer is not always truer" and "the latest is not necessarily the greatest." The biblical faithful who cringe at our *"carpe diem"* effrontery toward the millions of the world's poor can still learn in back-handed fashion from the self-indulgent that it is good to be content with one's straits (Philippians 4:11), but also to be joyful with "Amens!" for the gifts God puts in our laps (Psalm 136, the sevenfold refrain of Ecclesiastes). And Bible-believing Christians who are grateful that God's will is *not* hidden but is fully revealed in the person and Way of Jesus Christ (Deuteronomy 30:11–20, Colossians 3:1–4:6) can learn from a Jungian mythologizing perspective that there may be more about us humans than is dreamed of in many a rigid orthodox theology.

That is, by "antisympathetic vibration" (Seerveld 1995/1962, 20), to extend John Calvin's (1509–1564) metaphor of Scriptural eyeglasses (*Institutes of the Christian Religion* I, 5, 14), Christians with a biblically Christian, committed world-and-life vision are free to receive instruction from those who are confined to bad neighborhoods, because world-and-life visions are *relatively important*—they are not the pearl of great price (Matthew 13:45–46). And followers of the Lord Jesus with a steady vision of creatures *coram Deo* headed for the *eschaton* of Jesus Christ's return may also be able to *give* a corner of *vision* to those who may still be looking. It is not that a biblically Christian world-and-life vision claims to be more or the most "rational" world-and-life vision available, because *visions* are imaginative fabrics and not provable or disprovable by arguments (Griffioen 1989, 87). Christians may *give away* insights F.O.B. Be winsome with your wisdom, says Scripture (Colossians 4:5–6), and make those with poor eyesight and handicapped hearing jealous to envision the shalom you present amid a cloud of witnesses to God's providential mercy.

2. Different Christian world-and-life visions are still bound to submit to one Holy Spirit

The second implication that I want to draw from the fundamental distinction of *structural vision* and *directional mission*, which are always conjunctive, is a matter becoming more and more accepted in recent decades: *there are quite different committed Christian world-and-life visions* around; rather than "worldview" religious wars, maybe we need respectful cooperation in an apostate world culture where the Christian faith and way of life is no longer hegemonic but is fast becoming a minority position.

Whether one takes Richard Niebuhr's *Christ and Culture* (1951) taxonomy or David Naugle's more relaxed, rather churchly delineation of Protestant Evangelicalism, Roman Catholicism, and Eastern Orthodoxy (4–54), to which I should wish to add at least a couple more—the steadfast recurrent chiliastic wing of Christianity close to Anabaptist and Mennonite sensitivities and the definite community of "liberal" Christians focused on humanitarian needs, often named "the Social Gospel" movement and more recently "Liberation theology"—it is a fact that there are deeply cleft, long-standing Christian world-and-life visions that do not comport well and do aggravate one another.

Jesus' Solomonic judgment about why his followers were not ascetic in lifestyle as were Baptizer John's disciples is appropriate here: "Wisdom is justified by the deeds of *all* her children" (Luke 7:35; cf. Matthew 11:16–19). *Both* the wine-drinking Reformers *and* the Anabaptist "stepchildren" put the do-nothing caterwauling spectators to shame! So, rather than fight for dominance or submit the different Christian visions to arbitration to work out compromises, I suggest that we look to the alternate Christian world-and-life visions for wisdom to complement our own visionary lacunae or blind spots and take to heart that *all* of God's children fall under the stern injunction to be of one Holy Spirit (Romans 12:1–11, Ephesians 4:1–11).

I find it hard to take my own advice. It was great fun to bond with a Jesuit graduate student on the other side of the classroom at the University of Michigan in 1952 when he and I would challenge our brilliant Humanist professor Throop's exposition in a class on medieval societal history: that was a more enduring connection, I think, than when Communists and Calvinists worked together in the underground of Gestapo-occupied Netherlands.

My colleague George Vandervelde, who with a few dignitaries joined Pope John Paul II for after-supper prayers in his private Vatican chapel a few years ago, assured me the man is truly, phenomenally pious; but when I read the papal Easter Sunday 1999 letter to artists of the world with all its blatant Humanist blather about "artists . . . lead[ing] to that infinite Ocean of beauty where wonder becomes awe, exhilaration, unspeakable joy" (section 16)—good thing it is not written *ex cathedra!*— my supportive resolve weakens.

I remember that at the Jerusalem Synod, reported in Acts 15, it seemed good to the Holy Spirit and the brethren (v. 28) to remove circumcision from the essentials of the Christian faith; later, the apostle Paul was led by the Spirit to modify still further James's restriction on Christian non-Jews' eating food offered to false gods (1 Corinthians 8 and Acts 15:13–21). So, meanwhile, as different Christian world-and-life visions jostle with one another, I need to check first of all whether *my* spirit is holy and whether the witness of the Reformational Christian world-and-life vision to the truth is beyond reproach.

It might be wise to restore the shorthand formula often used to characterize this particular Christian world-and-life vision, in which I gratefully find myself at home, the full description Dooyeweerd gave *In the Twilight of Western Thought*: "the radical and central biblical theme of creation, fall into sin and redemption by Jesus Christ as the incarnate Word of God, *in the communion of the Holy Spirit*" (my emphasis, 42). A person could have an excellent Christian world-and-life vision, but if it be espoused with an ambitious, aggressive spirit, it is mere tintinabulating talk-show chatter or a clanging gong.

I do not expect a merger of committed Christian world-and-life visions, but I do believe the Lord asks us with our different Christian world-and-life visions to become one in the Spirit, with a unified witness to unbelievers and disbelievers testing out non-self-seeking *holy*.

3. *Cultural dynamics of evil principalities need special attention*

The third implication that I want to spell out for your response in thinking through the conjoined difference of *structured world-and-life vision* and *spirited direction/willed mission* is to be more definite and careful in delineating the ambit of world-and-life visions and in fathoming the locus and depth dimension of cultural turmoil.

The Holy Spirit is not a world-and-life vision but is God in person who mysteriously directs an obedient people toward shalom through tears. Principalities and powers are not a world-and-life vision but are uncanny perverse authorities "of the air," says Scripture enigmatically, evil "spirit(s) energizing persons right now into rebellion" (Ephesians 2:1–12). Unless we confuse the two, it makes sense to say: contrary world-and-life visions cause problems to their adherents because you need to translate what the other perceives, appraises, and hopes for into the shape of your own visionary perception, valuation, and expectation if you would understand what in God's world is being maintained by the other; but the opposition of spirits driving us human creatures and our deeds—which includes our world-and-life visionary constellations—entails outright war to life or death, no quarter sought or given. President George Bush, Billy Graham, the World Bank, the World Council of Churches, the city where I live, ordinary you and me ourselves are jackasses (*ceu iumentum*)—to use Martin Luther's (1483–1546) rough, colorful metaphor in debate with the erudite scholar Erasmus (c. 1466–1536) on how human willingness relates to God the Spirit and the Satan who contend to ride us willing creatures ("*De servo arbitrio*," *Werke*, Weimar Ausgabe 635: 23–28): we persons, communities, society with a mix of world-and-life visions are sites for mortal conflict between spirits that will drive us to fruitful cultivation of God's world or to desolation. *The root struggle and warfare in history is not between world-and-life visions but is one of spirited direction.* No wonder Scripture pleads with us double-minded (*dipsuchos*) followers of Jesus Christ at a loss as to which Way to go, to ask God for Holy Spirited wisdom on the direction to take (James 1:2–8, 3:13–18).

So-called "postmodernism," as I understand what this inadequate term refers to, is not a world-and-life vision but is a spirit. Spirits(!) *dunameis*, to use biblical terminology. And principalities, powers, thrones and dominions captivate people craftily, sift like Chicago fog on cat feet into the crevices of one's *mentalité*. It is seldom a frontal attack.

Duchamp's harmless urinal "Fountain" in the New York Armory Show of 1913, Dada hijinks in Switzerland during so-called World War I, later Beat Generation poetry and the aging Picasso's parodies of masterpieces in the Fifties, 1960s "happenings," punk rock from England in the 1970s, MTV, John Cage frequenting Toronto, Jeff Koons at the Tate, are all weathervanes of a surging "cultural atmospherics" that dissolves the rusty chains of Rationalistic constraints and denies historical continuities, a kind of soft, destructive, no-hands-at-the-wheel nihilism. Parody kills with a kiss.

And there is another sophisticated spirit I think that one can detect that has gained cultural strength, especially in the academy, since Arnold Schoenberg's (1874–1951) twelve-tone music, Malevitch (1878–1935) paintings, and later Rothko's (1903–1970) icons, which makes practically a fetish of theory as interminable language games, where the trick is to remain seriously suspended in thought, achieving a deferring, noncommittal reflection on reflecting, driven as it were to be fixed in Lacan's (1901–1981) mirror phase of misrecognition. Virtuality beckons one on, flickers as if it be reality.

The principality I am naming "soft nihilism" and the principality I try unhandily to finger as a spirit of "Zetetic Agnosticism" are formidable powers loose in our generations—the ones that critics often lump together, I think, as "postmodernism." But these principalities are not the only game in town, although it may be the only one many academics are playing. A most pervasive power out to control and ruin human lives today, including mine, is the durable Beast of Pragmatism.

In 1967, as a traveling Fulbright Scholar in Germany, my wife and I went to a meeting at the U.S. embassy in Berlin, and I was able to ask a midlevel embassy official, "Why did you let them build the Wall?" His reply was: "We sent all the info to Washington; they put the data in their computer banks, and the answer came back: if you stop the wall here, they will build it further back; if you try to stop the wall there, they will build it still further back; so, unless you are willing to risk total war with Russia, let them build the wall around Berlin."

That same blinding spirit of trusting scientific, planned, experimental techniques to provide the right results, to base policy, norms, and action on, *for now*, rules today, it seems to me, the shifting fortunes in the West of what Eisenhower long ago called "the Military Industrial Complex," and it is not postmodern. Wal-Mart has a metanarrative of utility and is driven by the Pragmatist spirit of "Grow for maximum profits." And the wholesale armament industry, whose chief supplier worldwide is the United States, is not postmodern but cruelly Pragmatistic: "If your current military power does not bring your country security, you can afford more, bigger, and better weaponry—*it works!*"

The thrust of this third strand of my drawing out implications is that we do well not to overvalue our discovery of important world-and-life visions and not to abstract their formatting human consciousness from being embedded in persons, groups, and institutions that are dated and located battlegrounds of principalities, powers, and the Holy Spirit. It can be shown historiographically—though I cannot do that here now (see Seerveld 1980, 1989)—that the European Renaissance (c. 1420–1520) and the historical Reformation (c. 1520–1650), that later the Enlightenment (c. 1715–1770) and later Positivism (c. 1820–1920) are not just names for historians' shoptalk, but are actually "invisible authorities," the power play events in which people with committed world-and-life visions live out their seventy or eighty years, principalities that are pertinent for retelling history and for assuming cultural leadership in a given generation.

One should not inflate ruling cultural principalities á la Hegel into a single monolithic *Zeitgeist* phase of Absolute Spirit: different cultural *dunameis* vie for human allegiance in the same chronological time frame. And there is no rationale, so far as I can discover, on why Pragmatism, for example, supplants, let's say, Positivism as a dominant cultural dynamics, unless there be a "logic" of idolatry—idols wear out—or maybe even evil spirits get tired and give way to another one of the Satan's legion . . . .

Would it make any difference in how you conceive world-and-life *visions* or alter where we should aim our marbles and gird for battle to *set* the younger generation's *consciousness* (cf. *nouthesia*, Ephesians 6:4), if we kept distinct in this conjunct reality the force of *spirited direction*?

Literary Biblical Underpinnings
to the Imaginative World-and-Life Vision of a Community

Before I mention a few temptations and blessings of a committed Christian world-and-life vision, to add up the damages in my title, I need to treat, however briefly, the biblical underpinnings of a Christian world-and-life vision. A Christian world-and-life vision, like a biblically Christian way of life, does not just drop out of heaven ready-made. Those who pick up a packaged Christian world-and-life vision on someone's say-so, learn the words, and are relieved to have more than a ragtag bag of bits and pieces—*bricolage*—to situate themselves, maybe even to complement a good homespun way of life, will only be fellow travelers with Christ's body until the hot sun comes out or the weeds overrun your packaged vision (cf. Matthew 13:1–23) if you do not spend time keeping your world-and-life vision pulsing fresh by hearing God speak in Scripture. Then your "vision" can become an "ideology," as Jim Olthuis reminds us (34), and you use it as a safety filter rather than as an ongoing explorative ultrasound detector of surprising realities.

Creation Regained: Biblical Basics for a Reformational Worldview (1985) by Al Wolters presents clearly the Christian world-and-life vision I heartily recommend investigating because it highlights God's revelation in *creation* and ties appropriating such disclosure to an underlying intimate *Bible knowledge*.

Let me throw into the conversation two considerations:

(1) The texture of a world-and-life vision is *literary, imaginative*. David Naugle's characterization reads "a semiotic system of *narrative signs*" (253, 291)—telltales vestiges, perhaps, of the Rationalistic Orr, Clark, and Henry penchant—but Naugle does emphasize the story character of a world-and-life vision (297–303). Sander Griffioen says it best for me: "a world-and-life vision is less dependent upon concepts than a philosophy, goes to work more suggestively and thus gives more leeway to the personal power of imagination, is less dependent upon a heavily technical terminology."[3]

I think that is right. That's why William David Romanowski[4] and Richard Middleton and Brian Walsh[5] can forcefully show how cinema and pop music culture are carriers par excellence of reigning world-and-life visions. World-and-life visions must not be propagated as simplified lay philosophy. Literature and artistry best embody the richly nuanced, deft, incisive, subtly connected insights of a world-and-life vision, which, when redemptive, can give luster, resilience, and incentive to one's daily walk.

(2) The biblical writings also have a *literary* texture. A very fine book by David Smith and John Shortt, *The Bible and the Task of Teaching* (2002), makes very convincing that the Bible—which is where the Holy Spirit particularly hangs out today—has the flexible, metaphorical distinguishing storied mark that allows God's Spirit to insinuate its godly wisdom into the silt of our consciousness. The Bible brings categorical

---

3   "Omdat een wereldbeschouwing (of levensbeschouwing) minder op begrippen is aangelegd dan een filosofie, suggestiever te werk gaat en dus meer aan de persoonlijke verbeeldingskracht overlaat, is ze minder afhankelijk van een breed gedeelde taal" (Griffioen 2003, 242).

4   *Pop Culture Wars* (1996), *Eyes Wide Open* (2001).

5   *The Transforming Vision* (1984); *Truth Is Stranger Than It Used to Be* (1995).

guidance intuitively rather than logically, scattering sparks of disciplined understanding, which piques further wonderment and keeps on percolating imaginative responses, as parables do. The Bible's historical accounts do not just provide "control beliefs" to double-check *post factum* what one supposes to be so, but gives us reliable imaginative apriori promissory horizons in which to be communally busy in God's world—and to teach students (59–60, 70–77, 87, 117–19).

Much more must be said, but a crucial plank in my argument for the inadmissibility of not constantly swimming in Scripture to keep one's Christian world-and-life vision alive rather than deadly formulaic—and I know there are many nominal Christian fish on dry land—is the fundamental conviction that God's written Word has the power to break through the historiocultural veils over our sinful eyes, whether inherited or recently adopted, and set us straight, open to God's call (cf. 2 Corinthians 3:12–18), *outfitting us with the vision of Jesus Christ's Rule acoming, so that our communal walk and our communal consciousness can be (fallibly) scripturally directed* rather than a church-going variant of the "normal" lifestyle, visions, and apostate powers so much in evidence.

I know this thesis is moot.[6] In his evaluation of Patristic culture, K. J. Popma asks honestly: both the Patristics and we ourselves want to ground our critique of culture biblically, but do we not speak with the accent of our crooked age as much as we may think the Patristics did of theirs? Even Christ's Church has, at times, in public made concordats with evil regimes! Yet Popma heartens my conviction by appealing to what he calls a basic "naive Bible-sense" (101–2, 105–8), what I would call a predogmatic, pretheo*logical* reading of Scripture, an historically and literarily aware listening on-your-knees reading of the Bible, swimming in it (Seerveld 2003, xii–xiii, 83–86), which allows God's Word to shatter the prejudiced visions we have picked up—what happened to St. Augustine when he finally reread Romans 13:13–14 (*Confessions* VIII, 12, 29), what turned Luther's world upside-down when he discovered *poenitentian agere* in Matthew 4:17 meant "repentance" instead of "penance" (Thesis 2), what can happen to us once we realize *torah* is the Redeeming Creator Lord's merciful covenantal embrace(!) rather than a big godly stick with which to knock us back into line. Holy Scripture

---

6   Cf. my discussion of Jacob Klapwijk's idea of "transformational philosophy" and the approach of *spoliatio Aegyptorum* in "Antiquity transumed and the Reformational Tradition," Robert Sweetman, ed., *In the Phrygian Mode: Neo-Calvinism, antiquity and the lamentations of reformational philosophy* (Lanham: University Press of America, 2007), 232–237.

as God's Word, *credo*, can convict us to believe *in* Jesus Christ as *kurios* (not just believe *that* so-and-so is true), *call us/outfit us* with survival gear (Ephesians 6:10–20) to be participants in God's reclamation project of world reconciliation (2 Corinthians 5:17–20), and *give* some the gift to *discern the spirits* of the age (1 Corinthians 12:4–11, v. 10).

Blessings and Unnecessary Damages
in Holding a Reformational Christian World-and-Life Vision

The not inconsiderable blessing of sharing in this evangelical Reformational Christian world-and-life vision continually being reformed and reconfirmed (not verified) by living with God's Spirit-breathed booked *chokmah* (2 Timothy 3:16–17)—those from other Christian faith traditions may speak for theirs—is that you are *conscious* of where you stand in God's world, where you are headed with your life, what kind of messed-up good environs constitutes your matrix and *modus operandi*, and what kind of Chaucerian company you probably will be keeping (1 Corinthians 1:26–29). That is, persons are blessed—some are more engaged than others—blessed by an integrated vision of what's going on in God's cosmic theatre, to use John Calvin's metaphor (*theatrum Dei, Institutes*, I, 6, 2), where many go through their seven stages of living; make their entrances and exits, to pick up Shakespeare's image (*As You Like It*, II, 7); and by God's Word and Spirit are given the wherewithal to persevere in "making the life of Jesus visible in our often decrepit bodies," as the apostle Paul puts it (2 Corinthians 4:1–11). A Reformational Christian world-and-life vision provides a person context with historic footing and prospects for fruitful service that consciously solidifies one's human identity and provides patience, joy, and strength to exercise hospitality to strangers. *It costs one's lifetime*, but the yoke fits the faithful well and the burden is light (Matthew 11:28–30).

The stability of *consciously* knowing roughly the scripturally inspired lay of God's world and the purpose of life within it can deeply offend people, other Christians, too, who may be living distracted lives or are not conscious of their way of life and are made to feel as though they are stupid or backsliders in the faith. A misstep here can cause a lot of damage in a community. Especially if one's Christian world-and-life vision becomes a cliché, is touted as the best thing since bottled spring water, or is believed to be a sign that the millennium is breaking—a mistake also made by Christ's original disciples (Luke 19:11–27), who did miracles but sometimes could *not* exorcize evil spirits (Matthew 17:14–21; Luke 10:17–20)! One's Christian world-and-life vision can be surreptitiously idolized, become a shibboleth, turn one's circle of compatriots into a Hadleyburg,[7] or serve as license to go hunt materialism, naturalism, spiritualism and then hang their taxidermied heads up like trophies in your den.

But such unseemly damages can be avoided if you realize that *your Christian world-and-life vision is a thetical orientation and not a judgmental condemnation, a program for doing good for the commonweal and not a plan of attack on enemies.* A Reformational Christian world-and-life vision, Sytze U. Zuidema taught us, provides "beginsels" (starting points), *not* [he made up the word] "endsipels" (final-line markings). Sander Griffioen and Bob Goudzwaard say it well: when you have a biblically Christian world-and-life vision guiding your way as an imaginative map, as you proceed, new vistas open up for redemptive deeds.[8] I take this to mean that a Christian world-and-life vision is not a cut-and-dried paradigm you can be cocksure about—one size fits all feet; it is also not just a tentative guess about what you should be duly hesitant. No, *the evangelical Reformational world-and-life vision I find to be an enriching, imaginative, path-finding project* worth working out and carrying on is as wary as a snake and as innocent, vulnerable as a dove (Matthew 10:16).

Counting Up the Real Costs of a Christian World-and-Life Vision

There are two very expensive costs built in to the project of developing a Christian world-and-life vision that I will mention in closing: (1) follow-through with sustained, communal, regenerative, reflective deed in society; and (2) practicing a prophetic bona fide Christian philosophical systematics in the academy while working with specialist scholars at the inner reformation of theoretical disciplines.

(1) Sidney Rooy goes to the less famous 1 John 3:16–18 to say that "spirituality" is a cop-out unless you give your lives for brothers and sisters in need. Rather than stare adoringly toward icons of God, go "secular," man or woman! (in the medieval Roman Catholic sense of the term): go work *in the world* of ignorance, perversity, and hypocrisy. Unless you are empathetically suffering along with hurting fellow believers, to say from

---

7   See Mark Twain's short story, "The Man Who Corrupted Hadleyburg" (1899).

8   "Het is het gaan van een weg die aan het individuele leven samenhang geeft. . . . vast blijft staan dat elk pad afzonderlijk een bepaalde 'logica' kent: op bepaalde stappen volgen andere. . . . toegegeven dat het huidige leven diffuser is dan voorheen. Maar zonder wegen kunnen we niet. In zoverre behouden ook levensbeschouwingen een oriënterende betekenis" (Griffioen 2003/1996, 193). "In een weg-georiënteerd beleid verruimt de weg zich namelijk onder het gaan: elke initieel genomen stap voegt de informatie toe die je nodig hebt om verdere stappen te kunnen nemen" (Goudzwaard 1999, 21).

your tower high and dry, "Shalom, shalom" is merely a slogan (2002, 147–48, 152).

I am not talking about 1960s protest groups and countercultural demonstrations against the WTO, but I am speaking for long-range intergenerational movements like the Christian Labour Association of Canada, the Citizens/Center for Public Justice (Canada and United States, www.cpj.ca; www.cpjustice.org), the Work Research Foundation in Canada (now known as Cardus—www.cardus.ca), which, in our differentiated society, take the time to regroup institutionally to posit reformative/restorative actions informed by the vision of *Basileia tou theou*, the Kingdom-Rule of God in which, Gerda Hoekveld-Meyer says, there are no rights—only the duty of just-doing (1998, 64). God's people do not need to be successful entrepreneurs and political leaders so much as faithful at instituting protective, generous, healing deeds in society, especially for the impoverished. Even lone individual persons in legislative office or corporations need communal support if they are trying to end the fiasco of privatized faith. If we followers of the Christ are busy fashioning a salty Christian world-and-life vision in whatever circles of society we find ourselves, it behooves us not to default on putting the brave words into reliable deeds (1 John 3:18, James 1:22–25, 2:14–26).

(2) A Christian world-and-life vision is not theoretically precise enough to capture the "limiting concepts" that analytically determine the terrain for special scientific study of biology, for example, psychology, jurisprudence or . . . theology. It takes hyperconscious, philosophically exacting concepts and technical terms, not metaphors, to approximate the structural insights needed to break into the cycle of experience so one can order what is perceived and scrupulously relate finely drawn distinctions. "Modal aspects of things," "anticipatory and retroflective moments," "kernels of meaning," "limited sphere of authority," and "subsidiarity" do not make good storytelling; but jargon matching meticulous analysis is the meat of theoretical dissection, and such severe, logical abstraction is necessary to investigate the joists where specialized fields of scientific investigation interlock and expose the foci where one's faith orientation makes a difference. Henk Aay has shown how Christian geography scholarship in the Netherlands missed the opportunity to deepen its field of study with sociography because the professionals lacked the theoretical acumen to formulate Christian categories that could prevent transforming geographic science into ethnography (1998, 120–22).

Please do not misunderstand me. Making a Christian world-and-life vision winsome in the academy is of capital importance. And scholars specializing in world-and-life vision studies should actively seek to engage especially teachers of literature, art, and music history in the endeavor, because the intersection of world-and-life visions and period principalities are veritably palpable in the poetry, novels, paintings, songs, and symphonies to be studied in college, and professors in "the humanities" can train students to find good knowledge of God's world in slanted perspectives. Literary studies and interpretation of artworks are as rigorous and fine-tuned as philosophy, but they are just two different universes of discourse, in the way that reading Goethe's *Faust* intelligibly (1808/1832) is different from parsing Kant's *Kritik der Urteilskraft* (1790).

A phenomenal book like Ken Badley's *Worldviews: The Challenge of Choice* (Toronto: Urwin, 1996) is worth its weight in gold: this text reaches the high school(!) crowd mentality with cartoons, arresting typography, exquisite color photos, incisive commentary, and pointed questions that face teen-age youth with the incontrovertible truth that Muslims, Hindus, Buddhists, Sikhs, Jews, and Christians *choose* different understandings of family, work, technology, sexuality, medicine, suicide—Hey! What is *your* world-and-life vision, pardner?

This Christian world-and-life vision textbook is harder to write, I dare say, and perhaps a more effective Christian witness than many a finely argued treatise on apologetics. I am reminded of Bill Rowe's trenchant remark: when philosophy at the university lost its prophetic character and became professionalized in the last 100 years, the prophets went elsewhere (1989, 161). Maybe the prophets went into "worldview" studies!

But unless persons who value a Christian world-and-life vision support, request, and contribute to the formation of a *rigorous Christian philosophical systematics* that works through the categories needed to orient specialized theory of art, commerce, government, belief, health, language—you name it—the Christian community professing to give redemptive leadership in higher education has left off, in my judgment, building the tower of witness in the world Christ spoke of. Theoretical ideas do grow legs. And it is the proper task of *philosophy* to assist specialized theorists in conceiving original orienting hypotheses and in mediating the knowledge of detailed results into wisdom for life.

It is unfortunate, I think, when Christian scholars seem satisfied to promote a *theology* of art, theological psychotherapy, or a *theological* approach to politics, rather than a *Christian philosophical* examination in these disciplines. I support both formal and informal efforts to bring different brands of the Christian faith into a sound working relationship. But the academy needs something more fundamental than good will among church people and a sense of common mission to grapple with the troublesome thought-problem of sorting out the nature of "Christian philosophy" and "theological theory." My hunch is that this conceptual struggle goes back to radically different positions on the eucharistic Church at worship, the *corpus Christi* at large, and the Kingdom-Rule of God. My Reformational Christian faith-thought tradition is skittish about topping up disciplinary study with theological doctrinal control to make it kosher, particularly if it surfaces as a kind of Protestant clericalism. . . .

So as not to end on a querulous note, I'll relate a couple of incidents, comment, and refer to a photographic artwork.

In early 2003, Margaret Bendroth and Henry Luttikhuizen curated an art exhibit of paintings and prints at Calvin College in Grand Rapids entitled *The House of God: Religious Observation within American Protestant Homes.* Philosopher John Hare told me of being present in the gallery when persons who had driven hundreds of miles came to stand motionless in front of Werner Sallman's well-known *Head of Christ* (1940) and unabashedly began to weep in respectful silent devotion.

I recently visited Casino Rama, built and operated on native land in Ontario. In a huge cavernous amphitheatre filled with rows upon rows of packed-together slot machines, jingle jangling with exciting noises, colored lights flashing everywhere almost psychedelically, single individuals, some appearing dazed, often slumped in chairs, dropped loonies into slots and pushed buttons of rolling tumblers. Over in a quieter section around multiple ornate tables, tense, sharp-eyed persons placed bets down on a bouncing marble in a roulette wheel or on a few slickly dealt cards. I marveled at the magician-like quicker-than-the-eye skill of the croupier to sweep away the chips and with a fast dance rhythm set up the next trick nonstop for people to lay down new bets on the inviting bright green soft felt tabletop. I spent a hell of an hour as voyeur there, speechless, flabbergasted, crying inside at what appeared to me to be the public, humiliating exploitation of desperately lonely, unsatisfied neighbors of mine.

To complete the world and life picture on our hands, remember the distraught Muslim mother in Michael Moore's *Fahrenheit 9/11* film shouting/crying out to the heavens, "Allah akbar! Avenge this senseless destruction!" amid the smoldering rubble of her neighborhood homes and dismembered children. (I am afraid that the true God may be hearing her prayer.)

To become a disciple of Christ as student and educator is asking for trouble, a more severe judgment from God (James 3:1). It is a biblical norm for schooling, I believe, that the older ones serve the younger. A major task for Christian teachers is to offer and instill, God willing, in the rising generation, a biblically vital, redemptive world-and-life vision that has the horizons to encompass with compassionate meaning those served by pietist kitsch artistry, those addicted to gambling, and fervent, suffering theists who deny that Jesus Christ is the Son of God. Our calling from the Lord is to show and tell somehow to anybody who will look and listen—our students may be more poverty-stricken than they outwardly seem—that *to be inducted into the order of Melchizedek as priestly rulers following Jesus Christ* (Psalm 110; Hebrews 4:14–5:10, 7:15–28, 10:19–39; 1 Peter 2:9–10) *is the joyful crux of human life in God's world.* Our educative task is not to "empower" people, as I understand it, but to *give them the vision and the Spirited will to be diaconal.*

To avoid the damages of leaving tower-building half-finished and to capture the real cost of Christ's discipleship, I refer you, by way of example, to a series of five photographs by the Czech-American Duane Michals (born 1932), which plays loosely off "The Return of the Prodigal Son" (1982).[9] They illustrate metaphorically for me "the encounter" Johan van der Hoeven, glossing Buber, poses as a way to put a covenantal seal (1990, 27–29) on communicating and giving in a Holy Spirited way a Christian world-and-life vision off your biblical back to an other person in our ravaged environs.

The naked son, like a mirror image of Masaccio's Adam expelled from paradise, enters from the right into a room where the father is leisurely scanning *The New York Times.* The startled older man looks at the youth bowed in shame. The father loosens his shirt to protect the other's nakedness, and then thoughtfully removes all of his clothes to give them to the younger one. Finally, the naked old man gingerly gives the returned son a hug offering reconciliation.

I think such a gestural sequence may be a good image of how a Christian world-and-life vision gets transferred between generations. And the surprise in real life is that when you give somebody the visionary cloak of Christ's discipleship you yourself received once upon a time, when you help the other person put on the world-and-life vision God's Spirit has entrusted to you (Britt Wikstrom, *Caritas*, 2001), you *both* become clothed in the quiet glory of the Lord.

---

9   See, e.g., the Yale Art Gallery catalogue for the 1995 exhibition, organized by Ellen G. D'Oench, *Prodigal Son Narratives: 1480–1980.*

Select Bibliography

Aay, Henk. "Christian Worldview and Geography: Christian Schools in the Netherlands 1900–1960." *In Geography and Worldview: A Christian Reconnaissance,* edited by Henk Aay and Sander Griffioen, 108–24. Lanham: University Press of America, 1998.

Badley, Ken. *Worldviews: The Challenge of Choice.* Toronto: Irwin, 1996.

Curry-Roper, Janel M. "Christian Worldview and Geography: Positivism, Covenantal Relations, and the Importance of Place." In *Geography and Worldview: A Christian Reconnaissance,* edited by Henk Aay and Sander Griffioen, 49–60. Lanham: University Press of America, 1998.

de Graaff, Arnold H. *Psychology: Sensitive Openness and Appropriate Reactions.* Potchefstroom: Potchefstroom University for Christian Higher Education, 1980. 23pp.

Dooyeweerd, Herman. *In the Twilight of Western Thought: Studies in the Pretended Autonomy of Philosophical Thought.* Philadelphia: Presbyterian and Reformed, 1960.

Giamatti, A. Bartlett. *A Free and Ordered Space: The Real World of the University.* New York: Norton, 1988.

Goudzwaard, Bob. "Tussen de klippen door." In *Bewogen Realisme: Economie, cultuur, oecumene,* edited by Herman Noordegraaf and Sander Griffioen, 5–27. Kampen: Kok, 1999.

Griffioen, Sander. "Christian Higher Education in Europe: A Catholic View." *Christian Higher Education* 1: 2–3 (2002): 281–301.

———. "Is a Pluralist Ethos Possible?" *Philosophia Reformata* 59:1 (1994): 11–25.

———. "Kleine typologie van pluraliteit." In *Pluralisme, Cultuur-filosofische beschouwingen,* edited by Theo de Boer and Sander Griffioen, 204–26, 235–36. Amsterdam: Boom, 1995.

———. *Moed tot cultuur. Een actuele filosofie.* Amsterdam: Buijten en Schipperheijn Motief, 2003.

———. "Perspectives, Worldviews, Structures." In *Geography and Worldview: A Christian Reconnaissance,* edited by Henk Aay and Sander Griffioen, 125–43. Lanham: University Press of America, 1998.

———. *The Problem of Progress.* Sioux Center, IA: Dordt College Press, 1985.

———. "The Relevance of Dooyeweerd's Theory of Social Institutions." In *Christian Philosophy at the Close of the Twentieth Century: Assessment and Perspective,* edited by Sander Griffioen and Bert M. Balk, 139–58. Kampen: Kok, 1995.

———. "The Worldview Approach to Social Theory: Hazards and Benefits." In Marshall, et al., *Stained Glass*, 81–118.

———. "Tijd voor het levens-beschouwelijke debat." In *Aan Babels Stromen. Een bevrijdend perspectief op ethiek en techniek*, Feestbundel voor Egbert Schuurman, 118–29. Amsterdam: Buijten en Schipperheijn, 2003.

Griffioen, Sander, and Bert M. Balk, ed. *Christian Philosophy at the Close of the Twentieth Century: Assessment and Perspective*. Kampen: Kok, 1995.

Guinness, Os. "Mission Modernity: Seven Checkpoints on Mission in the Modern World." In *Faith and Modernity*, edited by Philip Sampson, Vinay Samuel, and Chris Sugden, 322–52. Oxford: Regnum Books, 1994.

Hoekveld, Gerard A. "Alien in a Foreign Land: Human Geography from the Perspective of Christian Citizenship." In *Geography and Worldview: A Christian Reconnaissance*, edited by Henk Aay and Sander Griffioen, 83–101. Lanham: University Press of America, 1998.

Hoekveld-Meyer, Gerda. "God's Own Countries? Contours of a Christian Worldview in Geography." In *Geography and Worldview: A Christian Reconnaissance*, edited by Henk Aay and Sander Griffioen, 61–82. Lanham: University Press of America, 1998.

Jenkins, Daniel. *Christian Maturity and the Theology of Success*. London: SCM, 1976.

Kienzler, Klaus. "Ist vom 'Christlichen' nur noch 'nach-christlich' zu reden?" *Wertepluralismus und Wertewandel heute*. Eine interdiziplinäre Veranstaltung zur 10-Jahres Feier der Universität Augsburg. München: Verlag Ernst Vögel, 1982. 3–16.

Klapwijk, Jacob. "Antithesis and Common Grace." In *Bringing into Captivity Every Thought: Capita Selecta in the History of Christian Evaluations of Non-Christian Philosophy*, edited by Jacob Klapwijk, Sander Griffioen, and Gerben Groenewoud, 169–90. Lanham: University Press of America, 1991.

Kok, John H. "To Have and to Hold: Peculiar Grounds for Cultural Engagement and Civil Disagreements." *Pro Rege* 31:1 (March 2003): 23–30.

———. "Vollenhoven and 'Scriptural Philosophy.'" *Philosophia Reformata* 53:2 (1988): 101–42.

Kuyper, Abraham. *Lectures on Calvinism* (1898). Grand Rapids: Eerdmans, 1961.

Marren-Reitsma, Heather. "Reading and Comprehension Strategies for

All Levels and Subjects." Session held for Northern Christian Schools Professional Development Day, Houston, British Columbia, Canada, 2 April 2004.

Marshall, Paul A., "Epilogue: On Faith and Social Science." In Marshall, et al., *Stained Glass*, 184–87.

Marshall, Paul A., Sander Griffioen, and Richard Mouw, ed., *Stained Glass: Worldviews and Social Science*. Lanham: University Press of America, 1989.

Mekkes, J. P. A. "Methodology and Practice." *Philosophia Reformata* 38 (1973): 77–83. [Original Dutch version: "Methodologie en Praxis." *Philosophia Reformata* 43 (1978): 3–10.]

Morrison, Toni. *Playing in the Dark: Whiteness and the Literary Imagination*. Cambridge: Harvard University Press, 1992.

Myers, Kenneth A. *All God's Children and Blue Suede Shoes: Christians and Popular Culture*. Westchester: Crossway, 1989.

Naugle, David K. *Worldview: The History of a Concept*. Grand Rapids: Eerdmans, 2002.

Olthuis, James H. "On Worldviews." In Marshall, et al., *Stained Glass*, 26–40.

Palmer, Parker J. *To Know as We Are Known: Education as a Spiritual Journey*. San Francisco: Harper, 1993.

Peck, John, and Charles Strohmer. *Uncommon Sense: God's Wisdom for Our Complex and Changing World*. Sevierville: The Wise Press, 2000.

Popma, K. J. "Patristic Evaluation of Culture." *Philosophia Reformata* 38 (1973): 97–113.

———. *De Universiteit: Idee en practijk*. Amsterdam: Buijten en Schipperheijn, 1969.

Rooy, Sidney H. "Education for Life: The Search for Wisdom in the Supermarket of Values." *Christian Higher Education* 1:2–3 (2002): 139–63.

Rowe, William. "Society After the Subject, Philosophy After the Worldview." In Marshall, et al., *Stained Glass*, 156–83.

Runner, H. Evan. "The Relation of the Bible to Learning." In *Christian Perspectives 1960*, 85–158. Pella, IA: Pella Publishing, 1960.

Seerveld, Calvin. "Does the World Ask Europe to Sacrifice its Beautiful Art?" In *The Art of Living*, edited by Jan Peter Balkenende, Roel Kuiper, and Leen La Riviére, 13–17. Rotterdam: CNV-Kunstenbond/Europäissches Zentrum für Arbeitsnehmerfragen, 2001.

———. "Footprints in the Snow." *Philosophia Reformata* 56:1 (1991): 1–34.

———. "Idealistic Philosophy in Checkmate: Neoclassical and Romantic Artistic Policy." *Studies in Voltaire and Eighteenth Century* 263 (1989): 467–72.

———. "Philosophy as Schooled Memory" (1982). In *In the Fields of the Lord*, edited by Craig Bartholomew, 84–89. Carlisle: Piquant, 2000.

———. "Reformational Christian Philosophy and Christian College Education." *Pro Rege* 30:3 (March 2002): 1–16.

———. *Skeleton to Philosophy 101*. Palos Heights, IL: Trinity Christian College, 1960. Mimeograph, iv–45.

———. "Toward a Cartographic Methodology for Art Historiography." *Journal of Aesthetics and Art Criticism* 39:2 (Winter 1980): 143–54.

———. *Why Should a University Exist?* Pusan: Kosin University Press, 2000. 80pp.

Sietsma, K. *De Ambtsgedachte*. Amsterdam: S. J. P. Bakker, n.d.

Smith, David I., and John Shortt. *The Bible and the Task of Teaching*. Nottingham: The Stapleford Centre, 2002.

Smith, James J. A. "Determined Violence: Derrida's Structural Religion." *The Journal of Religion* 78 (1998): 197–212.

Spykman, Gordon J. *Reformational Theology: A New Paradigm for Doing Dogmatics*. Grand Rapids: Eerdmans, 1992.

Strauss, Gideon. "A Nation of Idiots." *thINK* (Summer 2004), 1–2.

van der Hoeven, Johan. "Christian Philosophy at the End of the Twentieth Century." In *Christian Philosophy at the Close of the Twentieth Century: Assessment and Perspective*, edited by Sander Griffioen and Bert M. Balk, 55–66. Kampen: Kok, 1995.

———. "Development in the Light of Encounter." In *Norm and Context in the Social Sciences*, edited by Sander Griffioen and Jan Verhoogt, 23–25. Lanham: University Press of America, 1990.

Van Til, Henry R. *The Calvinistic Concept of Culture*. Grand Rapids: Baker Book House, 1959.

Wink, Walter. *Naming the Powers: The Language of Power in the New Testament*. Philadelphia: Fortress, 1984.

———. *Unmasking the Powers: The Invisible Forces that Determine Human Existence*. Philadelphia: Fortress, 1981.

Wolters, Albert M. "Dutch Neo-Calvinism: Worldview, Philosophy and Rationality." In *Rationality in the Calvinian Tradition*, edited by H. Hart, J. van der Hoeven, and N. Wolterstorff, 113–31. Lanham: University Press of America, 1983.

————. *Creation Regained: Biblical Basics for a Reformational Worldview* (1985). Carlisle: Paternoster, 1996.

————. "On the Idea of Worldview and its Relation to Philosophy." In Marshall, et al., *Stained Glass*, 14–25.

Zuidema, S. U. "Pragmatism." In *Christian Perspectives* 1961, 133–57. Hamilton: Guardian Publishing, 1961.

Part III
Worldviews: Before and After

"Where there is Love, there is Vision": Witnessing in/under/through worldviews

James H. Olthuis

"After Worldview" is an intriguing and challenging theme, especially for someone like myself, a neo-Calvinist who has spent his academic life emphasizing, promoting, one may even say, cherishing the importance of worldview. *After* often means "later than," "subsequent to," in the sense of "now that worldviews are passé, outmoded, modernist, what is next; what comes after in this postmodern world?"

On this read, I and all who emphasize the importance of worldviews could feel, how shall I put it, a tad defensive. At the same time, after meditating on this matter for the last months, I have come to realize just how rich the theme is. After all, talk about "after worldview" leads one to ask, what about "before" worldview? Moreover, *after* can also mean "intent on mastering," as "he is after your job." In this discussion, our conference would be about unearthing, making explicit, exploring, pinning down our worldviews. Less charitably, it could mean that we are going after each other's worldviews to show their inconsistencies or inadequacies.

Then again, less common, but no less intriguing, would be to read *after* in the sense of "following," "according to," "she follows after him," "he follows the Calvinist line (or the Baptist or the Marxist line)." In this sense, *after* would mean "attempting to be consistent in one's life with his/her worldview, following after it, living according to it." And our deliberation could dedicate itself to dealing with the dynamics of living according to worldviews—how easy or, more likely, how difficult it is to live lives consistent with our worldviews.

In other words, the word *after* can bear a variety of constructions and nuances. And it is in terms of all of this nuance that I want to make my comments. Indeed, I am not only going to be emphasizing "after world-view," but before worldview, in/under/through worldviews. My point will be double-edged. On the one hand, I will restate how indispensable, important, and necessary worldviews continue to be. On the other hand, I want to underline how dispensable, insignificant, and contingent worldviews, in fact, are. In other words, we are called to be jugglers, let us say, holy jugglers. Only, I am convinced, if we are able to help each other keep both of these balls in the air will we be able to be vigorous in championing our worldviews even as we honor and celebrate difference with all gentleness and humility. I will end by suggesting that most crucial for all of us, regardless of the details of our various worldviews, is the witness and testimony that is made in and through our worldviewing.

This also means that, I want to confess right at the outset that this is a very autobiographical paper. The way my argument unfolds and the conclusions it suggests are in sync with and resonant of my own long worldview journey with its struggles, shifts, and turns. Indeed, aware that I am speaking tonight at Cornerstone, a Baptist institution, brings back a memory to me about an experience that I had about forty-six or forty-seven years ago, when I was a student at Calvin College, and serves for me a most vivid indication of where I have been, the journey I am still on, and where I have arrived at least for the moment.

While a young student at Calvin, a number of friends and I for a while made a practice of attending Wealthy Street Baptist Church for the Sunday evening service. Dr. Fuller was an inspiring preacher, and his colorful antics on the pulpit were quite a draw for us more somber Reformed kids. I recall the experience as if yesterday. One Sunday evening, Dr. Fuller was in full flight. He had come down from the pulpit, handkerchief in hand, sobbing as he made his altar call.

I remember his eyes suddenly darting to the balcony where six or seven of us young men sat. The next thing I knew, the assistant pastor had ascended to the balcony and was touching my elbow. "Is it well with your soul?" he asked. At the moment, I do not quite recall whether my heart stopped beating or whether it starting beating wildly. I do remember vividly the cascading emotions. Discomfort: this is becoming too personal. Fear: I'm really not sure! Smugness: good thing we Calvinists do not put so much emphasis on something as unreliable as feelings. And, I have never forgotten, jealousy: what do they have that we, or at least I, do not have? Boy, it would be nice to feel that confidence.

I remember mumbling something to the preacher, and he moving on to my friends with the same question, "Is it well with your soul?"

However, instead of marching to the altar at the front as the ministers were hoping, we hightailed it out of there. I do not think that I ever went back. I do remember us guys nervously joking about our predicament. We never seriously discussed it together.

However, on some subterranean level, I think that for a long while, bolstered by my class in Reformed Doctrine as being the truest interpretation of the Gospel—we Reformed people had the biblical world-and-life view—I rationalized that since Calvinists emphasized God's sovereign election, there was no need to have the emotional conviction and assurance of Arminians. After all, it is only too clear that their theology is way off. Our confidence is in our orthodoxy, not in our feelings.

But looking back on these years of my life, I now realize that these rationalizations were really not very satisfactory. They did not succeed in covering over an emptiness in my heart. So no wonder when in 1957/1958 I ran into Evan Runner—or should I say, when Dr. Runner ran into me—I became enamored with a Reformationalist vision of life. Here at last, so I thought and felt, was an intellectually profound vision of life that when embraced stirred one's passions and gave meaning and purpose to life. So I became an outright, card-carrying Reformationalist, one of Runner's band. At the time, even though it was only too obvious that we were a very small minority at Calvin, there was precious little room to admit that it was possible to be true to the Gospel, even in its Reformed version, in a variety of ways and in a diversity of shapes. No, so went the dynamics of vindication, since we have the most consistent, world-embracing, and most faithful worldview, it is imperative that we soldier on pushing forward with our program for the reformation of scholarship and the reforming of society. So began my passion with worldviews and my conviction that the Reformational world-and-life view is, if not the only possible Christian worldview, at least the best, the least synthetic, most comprehensive, most consistent, most faithful; in short, a biblical panacea for the ills of our time.

Consequently, in 1968, I came back to Toronto after doing my graduate study at the Free University in Amsterdam and began teaching at the Institute of Christian Studies, which institution I am still with to the present. During the next fifteen years or so, the nature, makeup, and function of worldviews held my attention, culminating in my 1985 essay "On Worldviews." In that essay, I described a worldview (or vision of life) as "a framework or set of fundamental beliefs through which we view the world and our calling and future in it." A worldview is, I said, descriptively a vision of the world and, at the same time, prescriptively a vision for the world. Moreover, and of crucial import for me, was my growing realization that a worldview as a "medium of mediation and integration" is a dynamic, in-process nexus, born, motivated, shaped, sustained, and renovated in the simultaneity of a two-directional movement between faith commitment and all of the other modes of human experience. That still deserves to be underscored some twenty years later. Tonight, I do not wish to bore you through repetition. But if you have not yet come across the article, I do recommend it for your further reading.

Rereading it for this occasion, however, has brought to the fore a crucial matter that calls, I suggest, for much more consideration. Looking back, I realize that although it may be implicit in this earlier analysis, the article, while pointing out that worldviews are mediums of mediation between faith commitment and all of the other modes of human experience, does not call attention to—certainly does not linger with—the space or gap between faith confession and worldview formation, on the one side, and worldview formation and life practices on the other. Crossing these gaps or spaces is a multimodal translation process with inevitable "slippage" as differences in historical epochs, traditions, languages, and socioeconomic location, intermingled with matters of gender, genetic inheritance, personal developmental history, disposition, and temperament play their role in the choices that peoples in communities make and put into practice. In other words, traversing these gaps is inherently risky. It is always a precarious undertaking with no in-hand, divinely prescribed guarantees that either the "bridging" strategies or structures erected are or will be the right ones or the only ones.

In effect, the presence of the gaps indicates, on the one side, that sharing a common faith need not mean sharing the same worldview, and on the other side, that sharing the same worldview does not by any necessary logic lead to the same sociopoliticoeconomic policies, not to speak of common communal practices. On both sides of a worldview, so to speak, is slippage. Although the importance of this, not merely its peril, but particularly its challenge and promise, has become more and more evident to me in recent years—as I hope to make clear—I remember being painfully hit over the head with this reality in the late 1970s. In January and February of 1979, the Lutheran theologian Gustaf Wingren was a guest professor in a seminar at ICS that I conducted with Henry Vander Goot, who was then professor of theology at Calvin College. As the seminar wore on, it became very obvious that, although in the matter of worldview, Vander Goot and I were neo-Calvinists and Wingren was Lutheran, on any number of important social matters, Wingren and I stood over against Vander Goot.

It also was in the same year that Al Wolters, now a professor at Re-deemer College, and I were the major authors of a "unity" document at the Institute for Christian Studies. Again, as subsequent events made strikingly clear, sharing a worldview, even jointly articulating it, does not ensure agreement on the policy or implementation level. Societal policy and societal reform is not a simple practical application of a worldview. There is always slippage between the worldview and its societal enact-ments.

The peril and promise of the gap on the other side, between faith commitment and worldview, crystallized perhaps most markedly for me in a conversation with Gordon Spykman, professor of religion for many years at Calvin, a friend with whom I conducted two or three joint courses at the institute. Gord was responding to my "On Worldviews" article that I have referred to earlier. "Jim," he said, "Your analysis of worldviews in general may be right on. But it seems that you have forgotten that there is *the* biblical worldview." Things were never the same between us after that. By proposing that every worldview, including the Reformational one, is a human construction that can never be installed as the biblically prescribed one, I had, he feared, strayed from the Path of Truth. I do not think that he ever quite trusted me again.

This was painful for me, the more so because, paradoxically, or ironi-cally, if you will, the realization that every worldview, including the one that I fervently embraced and championed, was nevertheless a human construction bearing all of the marks of its time and shapers, was im-pressing upon me more deeply the biblical truth that we live by faith and not by sight—not even by the sight afforded by our worldview. Although we ought never to relent in our zeal to shape a biblically attuned world-view, we need to resist the temptation to canonize our worldview as the biblical worldview, the master key in contrast to all others. In humility of spirit, we are then in a better position, not only to be thankful for our worldview and the dimensions of the Gospel that it highlights, but at the same time, to be open to, honor, and celebrate the angles of vision afforded by other quite different worldviews. Along these lines, we can hold on to each other in faith, mutually acknowledging and learning, even as we recognize that in this life we all see through a glass darkly.

When any group too closely identifies its worldview with the Gos-pel, there is not only an ever-present temptation to adopt a superior us-them mentality, but equally damaging, the worldview can easily act as a control mechanism that leads one to deemphasize, neglect, or underplay scriptural teaching. Again, a personal experience brought home to me just how negatively this can work itself out. It was in the 1980s, and one Sunday night I was preaching in a Christian Reformed church about how in the Pentecost Spirit, the early Christian community lived together, owning everything in common. As described in Acts 2:44–45, the faithful "sold their goods and possessions and shared the proceeds among themselves according to what each one needed" (The Jerusalem Bible). I was about halfway into my sermon when a man stood up and said, "This is a Reformed Church. If you want to preach about the Spirit, there is a Pentecostal church down the street" and proceeded to walk out, followed by about ten or fifteen others. I was flabbergasted and broke into tears on the pulpit. My point is not that the Reformed worldview leaves out the Spirit. That is certainly not true. I do believe, however, that (whatever the reasons) there is afoot, at least in the populace at large, an understanding that whereas emphasis on the Word is Reformed, emphasis on the Spirit is Pentecostal. And in this context, besides lamenting the fact that a fellow believer was able to feel that he was just stating the obvious, I am calling attention to the way worldviews, if they are baptized as the Truth, begin to function as ideologies, control mechanisms that not only exclude all that is different, but regard anything different as hostile and threatening.

Gordon Spykman's worry that I, in a certain way, was underplaying the importance of worldviews, certainly of the Reformational worldview was, curiously enough, countered by a concern that I was still overplaying the role and importance of worldviews. At least, that is I how I read Nicholas Wolterstorff's response to my paper when I presented it at a conference on worldviews held at Calvin College in the early 1980s. At the time, he said that, although he was basically in agreement with my central themes, he nevertheless thought that I still had a too thickly textured (idea of) worldview. I did not really know what to make of his critique, as my effort to describe the anatomy of a worldview had resulted in what I took to be a nuancing and relativizing—one could say in a certain way, a thinning down—of the import, place, and role of worldviews.

Now, some twenty years later, I think Wolterstorff was on to something. I now have a sense of what he was getting at, or, at least, I know what I would mean by calling my earlier view "too thickly textured." For, even though I relativized a worldview by situating it as a medium always informed and shaped in a two-directional movement between faith commitment and all of the other dimensions of human life, a worldview still has too much the feel of a more or less polished instrument, a kind of concrete and steel bridge, a pair of glasses that, if kept rightly ground, will allow its wearers to make sense of life, giving definite shape and form to the often murky and confused world of experiences that is reality.

Yes, I did highlight the reality that "sometimes, however, the world-view-experience gap remains unbridged" and people are thrown into worldview crisis. But that is described as an emergency, a "sometime" experience—an experience we hope will never befall us. Implicit, as I now read it, is the idea that if we can properly attend to the admittedly complex dynamics of giving form and shape to our worldviews, we will be able to erect a viaduct that succeeds in virtually bridging the gap between vision and reality. "Whenever there is a gap between vision and reality," I said, "there is crisis, frustration, and tension." I went on, "Unless people are able to refocus and make sense of reality again . . . they are likely to suffer breakdown."

Today, some twenty years later, I welcome the opportunity to present a different take on this state of affairs. Now, I envision worldviews not so much as structures that succeed in bridging the gap, but as rope catwalks, suspended foot-bridges that, although allowing us to traverse the gap, never remove it and never let us forget that crossing it is accomplished in the risk of faith. In other words, there is no one correct, biblical worldview; no worldview is a panacea that, if applied strictly and consistently, removes or resolves the difficulties of life. It is not that when we have a good-enough worldview, the gap is bridged and we are free of "crisis, frustration, and tension." Rather, the difficulties and messiness of life are always with us in this life, as will be crisis, frustration, and tension. The challenge is, rather, to accept the difficulty, tension, and struggle of life as normal and to construct, inhabit, and employ the best possible worldviews in concert with others as coping strategies, lines of approach, organizing schemas. In this faith posture, we are well positioned not only to adopt and adapt the worldviews we inherit, but to remain open to other worldviews, learn from them, work with them, in the process learning to honor and celebrate difference not as threat but as invitation.

There is also one other very important benefit that accrues with such a reframing that I would be amiss not to mention. Very often—too often, from my experience as teacher and psychotherapist—when we overplay or overload our worldview as the formula which, if properly and zealously followed, ensures a God-honoring life, people of faith lose themselves in guilt or depression or drown in feelings of self-loathing, shame, or inadequacy when things do not proceed as planned. They were given the right worldview, but somehow things have not worked out. So they must be unworthy, God must be punishing them, or they must be people of little faith. When, on the other hand, we are able to work with our worldviews as helpful and trusty guidelines—in distinction from detailed blueprints or dyed-in-the-wool instructions—we have the inner and outer space to more fully appreciate that a life of faith cannot be programmed and that the doubts, risks, uncertainties, disappointments, and calamities that come our way are part and parcel of human life, without immediately experiencing such setbacks as signs of disobedience and unbelief, with all of the attendant and concomitant feelings of self-deflation or -inflation, shame, guilt, or whatever.

All this means that today, I would entitle my article "On World Viewing" instead of "On Worldviews." The emphasis would be on the ongoing, faith-infused, dynamic activity called worldviewing with the resulting worldviews always in process/on trial—less "thick," it could be said.

Focusing on world viewing brings into purview the complex dynamics of sight. Developing one's ability to see is a learned developmental process. When, as a young infant, I feel that I am seen as lovable and worthy, I begin to see myself in the same light and I feel affirmed and loved. "I am seen [loved], therefore, I am" (rather than Descartes' credo, "I think, therefore, I am")—and seen, I am open to see the world and others. However, when things go seriously wrong developmentally, my ability to see becomes emotionally clouded and obscured. Both how I see myself and how I view the world is negatively affected.

Simultaneous and interconnected with perceiving myself and the world, I distinguish and think. Perceptions and conceptions mutually interact. I begin to see what I think and think what I see. In the period of modernism that developed in the West after Descartes, world-and-life views developed under the primacy of intellectual thematization. World perceptions were identified with/transformed into world conceptions, worldviews emerged as a framework of conceptualized beliefs.

Today, with the demise of foundationalism, it is increasingly being recognized that since worldviews call upon a universality that cannot be rationally grasped, presented, or demonstrated, but can only be pointed at and affirmed in the witness of faith, they are more unreasoned hunches than reasoned conclusions. For the most part, however, worldview as an idea is still very intellectual and rational. As is more and more being accepted and understood in our postmodern world, in the West, we have theoretically given pride of place to sight and intellect (and thus worldviews) at the cost of the other senses. Indeed, as I read it, a major question for us at this conference is whether the worldview ship can be pried loose from its intellectual moorings and retooled to do service in the often uncharted and tempestuous seas of faith and life.

My wager in response to this question is this: When world viewing is accented as fundamentally an activity of faith (in which faith perceptions are patterned into coherent and cohesive frames for viewing life), worldview is still a serviceable concept—albeit as a canoe or sailboat rather than a destroyer or ocean liner. For me, this involves giving due place and honor to nonrational ways of knowing in the formation and function of worldviews. As soon as we understand world viewing as an activity of faith, attention is called to the very real presence of these nonrational modes in the life of faith as well as life in general. In addition to worldviewing, there is what I call world feeling, world touching, world smelling, world tasting, world hearing—all of which, in interactive intertwinement with each other, play their crucially distinctive role in influencing and shaping the worldviews we adopt and the lives we lead.

Deep down we can feel at home in the world or not at home. We can experience the world oysterlike, or we can be terrified. We yearn to touch and be touched, to feel in contact, be connected. Feeling in touch with self, others, God, and the world is like heaven; feeling out of touch or hurtfully touched is hellish.

Our sense of smell often provides the first indication that something is rotten in the State of Denmark. It was Nietzsche, I think, who first proposed a smell test for philosophy. I am sure that we all have a good sense of what he meant. We can hear someone talk, all the words can be there, but we do not quite trust it because we smell a rat. Taste tells us when something is bitter and when it is sweet. Terrible food can taste oh so good among friends. Bad experiences can rob us of our appetite. We can be in awe of a most persuasive argument, and yet, because we are left with a sour taste in our mouth, we remain unconvinced. We are told, in Scripture, to taste and see that the Lord is good. To feel heard creates the ability and desire to listen to others, just as feeling unheard leaves one isolated, unable to be genuinely open to listening to others. The sound, tone, and modulation—what Kristeva refers to as the semiotic dimension of language—makes all of the difference in what we hear. Many of us become adept in "putting our ear to the ground," listening for what is really being said, alert for any dissonance between the spoken words and its underlying message.

We can go on and on in this vein. All of these sense-oriented fundamental moods, patternings, predilections, abilities, or intuitions formed in our early childhood experience play an indispensable and inextricable role in life and in worldview formation. In concert (with all kinds of variation and intensity, as typically some sensory abilities are more highly developed than others in most people) these ways of knowing play their role in shaping and giving support to a vision of life that both gives credence to and makes room for these honed abilities, even as it assists in making sense of and illuminating such sensory wisdom. If early formation is good enough, there will usually be a good-enough, continually recalibrating, mutually interactive fit between the adopted worldview and sensory knowledge. However, if early experience is replete with experiences of abandonment, trauma, and abuse, the sensory panoply of abilities will suffer defensive maldevelopment (such that, for example, one hears, sees, smells danger everywhere). In such situations, afraid, unable to be open to the world, people, understandably, tend to adopt worldviews that justify their take on the world. At the same time, if such people find themselves in a community of faith that has a life-affirming worldview, they are offered a vision to which they can turn for healing and support. However, as I mentioned earlier, if the early emotional damage is not adequately attended to, such people can often be thrown into bouts of depression, shame, or numbness, unable to feel good about themselves, angry, unable to live according to the faith they confess. I have to leave this without further development. Here, I have no doubt, are vast new arenas for further exploration.

My point in all of this is to propose that there are good reasons to amend my earlier description of a worldview "as a medium of mediation and integration in a two-way movement between the commitment of faith and all of the other modes of human experience." Now, I want to suggest that a worldview is more adequately described as a comedium of mediation and integration in concert with all of the other ways of sensory knowing.

As I draw this address to an end, I want to share with you one other recent experience and make a few comments. A year ago, at the behest of Jamie Smith and myself, there was a conference at Calvin College that brought leading advocates of Radical Orthodoxy (hereafter RO) in conversation with a number of Calvinists of various persuasions. Two weeks ago, Jamie Smith submitted an edited book manuscript of this conference to Baker. I wrote an Afterward in the volume, in which I mused on the irony of the fact that although both groupings are exceptionally zealous in their enthusiasm for God and the coming of God's Kingdom on this earth, one in their critique of modernism's neutrality, in many respects, their worldviews are quite different from each other. Reformationalists (hereafter RT) like myself tend to get squeamish when we hear ROs talk of finite participation in the infinite. We are afraid that such participation, even if only analogically, blurs the creator/creature distinction, infringes on God's sanctity, and calls into question creational goodness.

On the other hand, ROs are rather quick to dismiss Calvinism (and Lutheranism) as aiding and abetting modernity's slide into nihilism. For ROs, anything less than "participation" is already, perforce, to grant too much independence to creation.

The sad reality is—and, looking at the historical record, this seems, in general, the rule far more than the exception in the history of the church—both groupings are most often so invested in their own worldviews (along with their theoretically articulated paradigms) that these, in fact, become formidable wedges between the groups to the point of endangering their confessional solidarity—in which cases, the bitter intramural acrimony that typically breaks out badly tarnishes the witness of the Gospel in the world.

In that context, last year's conference was a wonderful success, as we discovered together that, in and through rather substantial differences, there was a very evident oneness of spirit and intention. Since then, one question in particular continues to haunt me: what can help us—one in Christ in the communion of the Spirit—the better to listen to and understand each other in and through our differences?

Musing on this situation, I have been struck by the realization that what each group perceives to be the logical outcome of the other's position is not necessarily true to that position. In other words, owning our fears in regard to each other would be a giant step toward creating a wonderful space of mutuality in which each group could both royally own the strengths of the other, honestly admit to the limitations of their own conceptualizations, and, at the same time, hold their own positions with poise and conviction.

Such a space of mutuality could open up, I want to suggest, if we would more intentionally recognize and attend to the gaps (without neglecting the interlacements) between faith commitment, worldviews, and their outworkings in both philosophic theories and everyday practice—the very same gaps to which we have already paid attention. We do well to see such "gaps" not as breaches that we declare bridged, but as between-spaces that—as faith deepens, insight grows, storms break out, times and conditions change—we negotiate our way through and over, ever aware that the translation protocols and procedures we employ are always in process/on trial.

Properly recognizing these gaps forces us to acknowledge the inescapability of some slippage as we move back and forth between the testimonies of faith, worldviews, and outworkings. Such slippage is, then, not something to be rued or papered over, but honored as underscoring the reality that in the vulnerability and awesome responsibility involved in translating faith into action via worldviews, we all would do well to learn from and interact with other groupings and other traditions.

The gain for us, I suggest, is immediate and most important. Suddenly, the pressure is lifted as to whether disagreement on the worldview (as well as on theological/theoretic) level necessarily or virtually implies that one party is unfaithful to the Gospel—with all of the accusations, counteraccusations, and acrimony that we are all too familiar with in the history of the Christian church. Vigorous discussion can take place without the tightness and intensity that can raise such interchanges to a fever pitch. Without the implicitly (often consciously) felt fear that if we open ourselves to new or alternative worldview formulations, we are thereby being unfaithful to the Gospel, interworldview or interparadigm discussions (theological, liturgical, and political) can be more playful, more creative—and in the process, I suggest, more gracious, more open to the leading of the Spirit.

A space of generosity and hospitality opens wide, enabling us to welcome and respect other traditions with their different worldviews. Paying close heed to the distinctiveness of testimony, worldview, and societal enactments allows the full-bodied testimonies of faith, the stirring declarations of worldviews, and attendant societal practices to, each in its own way, be considered, compared, critiqued, learned from in their mutual interlacement without either being identified, confused, or conflated with each other or reduced to each other. In brief, dwelling in the space that opens when we attend to the differences between faith confession, worldview articulation, and practical enactment allows us to expect, recognize, and legitimize conceptual, worldview, and paradigm diversity.

Returning to our case in point—the discussion between RO and RT—we are empowered to recognize that the differing paradigms of RO and RT are not so much competitors as alternate ways (with differing paradigms) of articulating our solidarity in the faith. Then, instead of a battle between opponents in the faith, we have the chance that a genuine discussion will break out in which each grouping is able to own more forthrightly the deeper fears/reasons for its preferential formulations and, at the same time, to acknowledge the fears/reasons that lead it to be wary of alternative conceptualizations.

When I look at RO and RT along these lines, something strange and paradoxical begins to emerge: both traditions seem to adopt their positions and reject the alternatives for precisely the same confessional desire, namely, to keep God and creation in intimate connection, while honoring their difference. While RTs tend to be worried that RO talk about both God and creation in terms of participation and analogy too easily leads either to considering that creation has some existence on its own or to a downplaying of the excellence that belongs to creatures of flesh and blood, ROs are clearly worried that the dynamic of RT allows for too large a distance between God and creation ending in a Deism and even prepares the way for nihilism. Although the similarity of the fears (as well as the underlying intentions) may not be all that surprising to many, the more I take them in, the more I feel myself moved to a deeper sense of appreciation for RO, more ready to listen and learn than to refute and resist.

Attending to the worldview/faith commitment gap not only creates space for better communication, understanding, and cooperation between people of the same faith, but on the broader scale, it also opens up, encourages, and fosters cross-cultural communication, interfaith understanding, transparadigm connection. Instead of being limited—and generally frustrated and stymied—by trying to find each other in terms of and via very different, sometimes diametrically opposed worldviews, we are invited to listen for and to the witness of faith, murmurs of the heart, groanings of the spirit that sound through in/under/through the worldviews. Cocking our ear and listening for what is being witnessed to and confessed (in and through words, views, and concepts that are very strange or upsetting) is an act of respect and vigilance—I call it suffering love—that can lead to the miracle of connection.

Indeed, since we all live by faith and not sight, whatever our worldview, whatever our faith, in the end, our efforts to reach each other and connect are acts of faith in which we witness and give testimony. Here, we say to each other, is how I feel/touch/taste/smell the world. This is what turns me on. This what upsets me. This is what I am convinced we need to do.

Across the abysses that divide us, witness calls to witness, testimony to testimony. Here, in testimony, witness, and confession, we extend invitations to each other beyond, below, and through our reasoned worldviews.

Consequently, just as we can be discomfited when we find ourselves wondering if people are only paying lip service in their witness or saddened when we experience ourselves to be fundamentally at odds in our testimonies, we can also, at times, experience the surprise and joy of connection and mutual understanding despite differences of worldview and faith.

This, in terms of a Christian worldview, a worldview that I espouse, makes all kind of sense. Life—creation—is God with us. Love. Humans as well as all of the other members of the creational family participate with God in the ongoing adventure in the wild spaces of love we call creation. In spite of sin and evil, Love—the love of God—is stronger than death, continuing not only to nourish and sustain us, but, in the gracious stirrings of the Spirit, surprising us in whom, how, and where it shows itself. May we have ears to hear and eyes to see.

Ubi amor, ibi oculus. Where there is Love, there is vision.

Response to James Olthuis

Craig E. Mattson

I should like to suggest an image for Professor Olthuis's worldview-ing, one borrowed from Robert Frost's poem "Birches."

> When I see birches bend to left and right
> Across the lines of straighter darker trees,
> I like to think some boy's been swinging them.[1]

Olthuis sees worldviewers as swingers of birches that bend sometimes to the left and sometimes to the right and sometimes, in happy coincidence, toward other birch-swingers. I like this read on the worldview concept for reasons at least partially autobiographical. He begins his paper with a story of an encounter with some Baptists, which is where my own story began—born, bred, and blood-bought in fundamentalism. Although he found them enthusiastic, my own church experience was significantly different, framed as it was in what Frost might call a line of straighter, darker trees. Olthuis's self-deprecating remarks notwithstanding, his re-ligious tradition does not have a corner on rigidity; enthusiasts, too, can be wooden thinkers. As a counter to the intellectual rigidity that appears even in an anti-intellectual tradition, Olthuis's playful take on world-views offers "the gaiety that goes with all true thought."[2]

Olthuis's birch swinging is energized by a critique of visualist ways of knowing. Although he does not cite Walter Ong, Olthuis's explorations of olfactory, gustatory, and aural analogies echo Ong's scholarship on the "sensorium," the prioritizing of the various senses and their attendant sensory analogies for our knowledge of the world.[3] Modernity's episte-mology has largely depended on visualist terms—*composition, definition,*

---

1   *The Poetry of Robert Frost*, ed. Edward Connery Latham (New York: Holt, Rinehart, 1969), 121.
2   Vicki Hearne, *Adam's Task: Calling Animals by Name* (New York: Vintage, 1982), 87.
3   See Ong's *The Presence of the Word* (New Haven: Yale University, 1967) and *Ramus, Method, and the Decline of Dialogue* (Cambridge: Harvard University, 1958).

implication, description—that depend on "an analogy between the field of intellectual activity and a field which involves local motion and is sensorily apprehended in terms of sight."[4] Despite the ocular turn of the Enlightenment, however, the visual is not so basic for modernist epistemology as the tactile. "By touch," explains Ong, "we assure ourselves that the stone is there, is objective, for, more than other senses, touch indeed attests to existence which is objective in the sense of real-but-not-me."[5] This helps explain why Olthuis's analogies for worldviewing draw on the spatial and the tactile: gaps, slippage, catwalks, abysses, and the wild spaces of love. This linkage of visual and tactile analogies highlights the objectivist and interpretivist poles of the worldview concept: to look is to set something apart from oneself; to touch is to enter into relation.[6]

By making clear the sensory tendencies of modernist epistemology, Olthuis positions the worldview concept as one sensory mode among five, like the fingers on a hand. For moderns, epistemic analogies of sight and touch are as inevitable as our dependence on the retractable thumb and forefinger. We are always, so to speak, peering through our own "OK" sign to know the world we thus frame. Olthuis's talk of "world feeling, world touching, world smelling, world tasting, world hearing" acquaints us with a different sensorium whose analogies are as odd to us as a preference for the pinkie over the thumb.[7]

But despite the commonality shared by Olthuis and Ong, the two scholars diverge on their understanding of rational discourse. Whereas Ong plumps for a recovery of the classical rhetorical tradition in which the visual and the aural function cooperatively in reasoned exchange, Olthuis prefers nonrational discourse attentive to "the witness of faith, murmurs of the heart, groanings of the spirit," apparently on the grounds that traditional argumentation is contaminated by foundationalist epis-

---

4   Ong, *Ramus*, 107.

5   Ong, *Presence*, 169.

6   Ong, *Presence*, 173.

7   Whether these sensory analogies should be considered "non-rational," as Olthuis calls them, is another question. They may have a reasonableness characteristic of what Michael Polanyi calls the tacit dimension. That is, they may be vectoring toward explicit rationality, even if their logic begins in the inarticulable. As Wayne Booth explains, "[A]ny motive, however emotional or 'base' or 'animal,' can become a good reason—not necessarily decisive, but not irrational—simply by entering the consciousness, being weighed, along with other "reasons," and found to be essential or appropriate, no longer accidental, to the decision." *Modern Dogma and the Rhetoric of Assent* (Chicago: University of Chicago, 1974), 163.

temology. Contrarily, Ong connects visualist analogies not to the empirically committed tactile analogies of the Enlightenment but to the aural analogies of classical and biblical traditions. In short, he grounds rhetorical practice not in modernist epistemology, but in what Stephen Webb calls "acoustemology," which seeks to know the world in terms of the presence of the divine Word.[8]

In place of the classical norms of rhetorical civility, Olthuis presses for what might be called rhetorical hospitality. As I take it, the chief difference between the two is that whereas civility entails commitment in quest of reasoned articulation, hospitality tries to sustain solidarity by discursive virtuosity. His notion of worldviewing resolves itself throughout his essay into an image of people tossing brightly colored beliefs into the air and peering through the constellations formed in their tossing to see what they can make of the world. The upward-turned faces, the eager concentration, the mutual effort, the play of multicolored convictions— all of these make for lovely but daunting imagery. But this is no mere intellectual charity; here is an adept and gently ironic articulateness as well as an almost telepathic solidarity in quest of what he calls "the miracle of connection." "Holy jugglers," to use his term, "royally own the strengths of the other, honestly admit to the limitations of their own conceptualizations, and, at the same time, hold their own positions with poise and conviction." I am reminded of the P. G. Wodehouse story in which a hung-over Bertie Wooster looks up from his girlfriend's favorite book on ethical theory and remarks, "All perfectly true, no doubt; but not the sort of thing to spring on a lad with a morning head."

To note the difficulty of the kind of exchange Olthuis proposes is, of course, not strictly an argument against it. For birch swingers, there always comes a point when, after having kept his poise

> To the top branches, climbing carefully
> With the same pains you use to fill a cup
> Up to the brim, and even above the brim . . ."

the boy flings himself "outward, feet first, with a swish, / Kicking his way down through the air to the ground."[9]   But Olthuis's worldviewing, despite its nonintellectualist stance, may be inadvertently exclusivist in that it requires a mastery of discursive competencies generally restricted to social conditions leisurely enough to permit redescriptive play. Some civic exigencies, however, may forbid this sort of ludic discourse. Will

---

8   Stephen Webb, *The Divine Voice* (Grand Rapids: Brazos, 2004).
9   Frost, *Poetry*, 122.

Olthuis's "unreasoned hunches" achieve rhetorical traction in arenas of dire poverty, corporate sophistry, or nationalist bloviation?[10]

Here is a hunch of my own: Olthuis's downplaying of traditional argumentation springs from a rhetorical miscalculation. He assumes that worldviewers are generally given to overconfidence. In some cases, they indubitably are. But R. R. Reno spots some cues that suggest that the malaise of our day is not Promethean, but Petronian—Petronius being the first-century Roman author of the clever but flippant and morally imperturbable *Satyricon*.[11] In this reading, our trouble is less likely to be arrogance than a certain moral and intellectual apathy,[12] which suggests not so much slippage between confession and worldview and practice as the disposability of all three.[13] Olthuis's call for ludic dialogue may abet the ironist habits now abroad.

Of course, playfulness offers new vantage points, cultivates humility, and honors human freedom. As Frost says, one could do worse than be a swinger of birches. But worldviewers need not only what A. J. Conyers calls an *elective*, but also a *vocational* understanding of reality.[14] That is, we need a calling from outside ourselves, so that, as W. H. Auden puts it, "for the first time in our lives we hear, not the sounds which, as born actors, we have hitherto condescended to use as an excellent vehicle for displaying our personalities and looks, but the real Word which is our only *raison*

---

10   I am grateful to Brian Walsh, whose critique of my response paper at the 2004 After Worldview conference educed this point from my original, much less focused observations about Olthuis's distrust of traditional argument.

11   R. R. Reno, "American Satyricon," *First Things* 116 (October 2001): 35–41.

12   John Durham Peters, *Speaking into the Air* (Chicago: University of Chicago, 1999), 35. This book offers some rationale for claiming that today there may be less danger of arrogance in the message sender than a certain moral and intellectual anemia in the receiver.

13   Perhaps nothing contributes to this disposability quite so much as what sociologists Abercrombie and Longhurst call the "mediascape," described in their fine book *Audiences* ([Thousand Oaks, CA: Sage, 1998], 37). As Todd Gitlin has pointed out, this pervasive mediascape cultivates "a relentless pace, a pattern of interruption, a pressure towards unseriousness, a readiness for sensation, an anticipation of the next new thing" (*Media Unlimited: How the Torrent of Images and Sounds Overwhelms Our Lives* [New York: Owl, 2002], 7).

14   A. J. Conyers, "Can Postmodernism Be Used as a Template for Christian Theology?" *Christian Scholars Review* 33:3 (Spring 2004): 293–309.

d'etre."[15] Here is a Word so authoritative that its aptest echo may be not winsomely ironic exchanges, but rather carefully reasoned, properly confident argumentation.[16] Such discourse honors not only the description and prescription afforded by a biblical worldview, but also the conscription that burned in the bones of cranky prophets, even when their countrymen were ever hearing and never understanding, ever seeing and never perceiving.

15 W. H. Auden, "The Sea and the Mirror," *For the Time Being* (London: Faber and Faber, 1953), 58.
16 Leslie Newbigin, *Proper Confidence: Faith, Doubt and Certainty in Christian Discipleship* (Grand Rapids: Eerdmans, 1995).

Appropriating *Weltanschauung*: On Jerusalem's Speaking the Language of Athens

ALBERT WOLTERS

Let me begin with an autobiographical comment. I grew up in a religious subculture—Dutch neo-Calvinism as transplanted to North America—where the phrase *world-and-life view* was often used to refer to one's overall orientation to reality at large, a phrase denoting something that had affinities with both philosophy and theology, but which was not reducible to either of these. In our circles, we liked to talk about the "Calvinistic world-and-life view," which distinguished our own particular tradition from other traditions, both Christian and non-Christian, and which had implications for all of life and culture, from education to worship, from labor relations to evangelism. My father was a strong proponent of this idea and not only taught it to his children, but also embodied it in his own life. He was a barber for most of his life—an occupation he would not have chosen if his life's circumstances had been different—and he was very serious about doing his barbering in the light of his Calvinistic world-and-life view. Among other things, this meant that he saw barbering as his divine vocation (despite his lifelong wish to be a teacher), that he took pride in his work, that he gave good value for money, and that he was honest in his advertising. It also meant that he engaged his customers in serious conversation about the issues of the day by relating them to his own and others' world-and-life view.

I myself later studied philosophy in the same tradition in which I had been raised and began to wonder about the historical roots of the category *world-and-life view* with which I had become so familiar. It was readily apparent that the term as used in my circles was a literal translation of the Dutch *levens- en wereldbeschouwing*, but this, in turn, proved to be a Dutch rendering of the German *Lebens- und Weltanschauung*, which had been popularized especially by the philosopher Wilhelm Dilthey around the turn of the twentieth century. As I began to dig deeper, I realized that this phrase was one of a constellation of expressions in German (others were *Weltansicht, Weltbild, Lebensanschauung, Welt- und Lebens-anschauung*) that clustered around the central notion of *Weltanschauung* or "worldview." When I had the opportunity to spend a sabbatical in the Netherlands in 1981–1982, I devoted part of my time to a project that traced the origin and development of the term *Weltanschauung* and its cognates. This part of my sabbatical research resulted in an unfinished manuscript entitled "*Weltanschauung* in the history of ideas: preliminary notes," which I never completed, since I moved from philosophy to biblical studies in 1984. I am delighted, however, that this unpublished and incomplete essay proved to be the germ and catalyst of the fine study by David Naugle on the concept of worldview.[1] Naugle's work does a much better job than I would have done in tracing the roots and ramifications of this seminal category in modern Western intellectual history.

My own transition twenty years ago from philosophy to biblical studies is also associated with the notion of worldview. In 1985, I published my little book *Creation Regained: Biblical Basics for a Reformational Worldview*, which arose out of an introductory philosophy course in which I used the category worldview as a means of linking a particular Christian philosophy with its biblical roots. In a way that far exceeded my expectations, this little book has served to introduce many Christians, not so much to the idea of a Christian philosophy as to the idea of a Christian *worldview*.

I mention these autobiographical facts to highlight a number of things. One is that I clearly have a lot invested in the concept of worldview. You might say that I have a good deal at stake in defending the legitimacy and viability of this concept, especially in a Christian context. Another is that, although I have been fairly intensively busy with the idea of worldview in an earlier phase of my academic career, it has not been central to my research and writing for some twenty years now. Consequently, like James Sire, I am revisiting a theme that played a key role in my earlier thought and writing and looking at it again with fresh eyes.

I have entitled my remarks "Appropriating *Weltanschauung*: On Jerusalem's Speaking the Language of Athens." It will be obvious to everyone that I am here alluding to the famous exclamation by the third-century church father Tertullian, "What does Jerusalem have to do with Athens?" in which Jerusalem stands for the biblical and Christian tradition and Athens for the tradition of pagan philosophical thought. Taking the

---

1   David Naugle, *Worldview: The History of a Concept* (Grand Rapids: Eerdmans, 2002).

terms somewhat more broadly, what I propose is to offer some general reflections on the issues involved in the adoption, within an explicitly Christian context, of key terms that have been developed outside of the Christian context and then to focus especially on *Weltanschauung* and its equivalents and translations as an example of such a key term. Ultimately, the question will be: is it spiritually and intellectually wise—and strategically prudent in terms of our present culture context—to speak of a Christian *Weltanschauung*/worldview?

To begin with, let me make it clear that I am talking about *key terms*, not just any word at all. It is clear that Christian discourse, if it is not to restrict itself to the biblical languages, will of necessity use a host of words and locutions that have acquired their meanings and associations outside of the circle of biblical revelation and explicitly Christian teaching, and that such use is not only necessary—not least for purposes of evangelism—but also largely unproblematic. There is nothing particularly problematic about Christians using the Arabic words for "tree," "green," or "throw." But matters get a bit more complicated when Christians consider using the key word *allah*, which is the ordinary Arabic word for "God." As is well known, Arabic-speaking Christians are divided over whether the word *allah* is so freighted with associations of Islamic religion that it cannot be legitimately used to refer to the Christian God.

As a matter of fact, the issue we are discussing would arise even if we were to restrict ourselves to the biblical languages, since even the vocabulary of biblical Hebrew, Aramaic, and Greek is embedded in the pagan cultures into which biblical revelation came. The book of Hosea uses the noun *ba'al* (Hosea 2:16) to refer to the God of the Jews, even though it was also the name of a pagan deity whose worship was proscribed, and the apostle John uses the word *logos* (John 1:1) to refer to the preincarnate Christ, even though it was a central concept in Stoic philosophy. On the other hand, the writers of biblical Greek could not bring themselves to use the regular Greek word for "altar," namely *bōmos*, to refer to the altar of the one true God, presumably because in ordinary Greek usage it was almost always used of the altars of pagan gods. So they coined a new Greek word, *thusiastērion*, to denote the altar of the true God.

However, the word for altar is an exception. Generally speaking, it is remarkable how free the New Testament writers are to use terms that had strong pagan overtones or that were intimately linked to the Greek philosophical tradition. Many Greek words that played a key role in Hellenic and Hellenistic philosophy are freely used in a nontechnical sense by the evangelists and apostles, without any suggestion of spiritual contamination because of these associations. Apart from the *logos* of the Prologue of John, we could mention a number of other striking examples: *anankē* (1 Corinthians 9:16), *nous* and *ta kathēkonta* (Romans 1:28), *hulē* (James 3:5), *theia phusis* (2 Peter 1:4), and *hubris* (Acts 27:10). It is a great mistake to read these terms as conveying the meaning that they bear in the tradition of Greek philosophical discourse. Thus, I would judge as utterly wrongheaded the New English Bible's translation of *nooumena* in Romans 1:20 as "visible . . . to the eye of reason" or the understanding of *theias koinōnoi phuseōs* in 2 Peter 1:4, commonly rendered "partakers of the divine nature," as referring to believers' ontological participation in the being of God.

Scriptural usage therefore seems to suggest that religiously alien vocabulary, including loaded terms from the extrabiblical intellectual tradition, can be converted to positive Christian use through being embedded in an alternative context, ultimately, of course, the context of the biblical metanarrative. At the same time, the example of *bōmos* and *thusiastērion* makes clear that there are also limits to this kind of positive convertibility. There is no positive New Testament use for the Greek *daimonion*, for example, or even *erōs*.

One conclusion that I draw from this is that language does not predetermine thought, that the so-called "Sapir-Whorf hypothesis" of the relation between language and thought cannot be validated in any strong sense. It is of interest to note in this connection that an early version of this hypothesis was defended in the early nineteenth century by Wilhelm von Humboldt, who argued that every language embodies a worldview (he used the German term *Weltanschauung*) and, therefore, that every speaker of that language thinks that worldview. On the contrary, it seems to be the case that entirely different worldviews can be expressed in the same language and to a large extent with the same vocabulary.

Nevertheless, it is also true that the Sapir-Whorf hypothesis is not without some justification. Not only is it difficult to translate certain concepts from one language into another (it is notoriously difficult, for example, to render the Dutch *gezelligheid* or the German *Gemütlichkeit* into English), so that it is difficult to *think* that concept in another language, but also, within the intellectual discourse of a single language, certain terms have become so strongly associated with specific schools of thought or traditions that they are virtually unusable for those who reject those schools or traditions. Thus the term *patriarchy* is contraband to those who do not wish to identify themselves with feminism, and the term *paganism* is taboo for those who want to distance themselves from traditional Christian orthodoxy. In an earlier age, the term *ideology* was connected so intimately with Marxism and the sociology of knowledge that it was almost always used in a negative sense, as a reflection of false consciousness or as a class-determined justification of the status quo, so that one would not use it to describe one's own commitments. (Nowadays, however, the term has lost those negative connotations in much academic writing and speaking.)

For Christian intellectuals, especially those working in traditions with a strong sense of the spiritual antithesis between biblical and unbiblical modes of thought, the issue of the legitimate Christian use of key categories forged in a pagan or humanistic environment becomes particularly acute. Thus, the Dutch neo-Calvinist philosopher Herman Dooyeweerd resolutely refuses to use the term *substance* in a positive sense, since in his view it always carries with it the connotation of something that exists in itself and that thus does not need anything else to exist. Since such a concept is antithetical to the biblical idea of creation, he rejected the term altogether. Hendrik Stoker, on the other hand, a philosopher who was in many ways sympathetic to Dooyeweerd's antithetical way of thinking, argued that the term *substance* was redeemable and could be used of an entity that was relatively independent within the context of dependent createdness. One could have similar arguments about the term *values* (to which I am personally allergic, because of its historicist roots), or *transcendental* (because of its association with an a priori human subjectivity that constitutes reality), or even *reason* (because of its association with rational autonomy).

The same issues surround the term *Weltanschauung* and its equivalents. Do its origins and the history of its use in modern intellectual history not militate against its usefulness as a prime Christian category? As I argued in an essay published in 1989, a strong case can be made for viewing the idea of *Weltanschauung* with a good deal of suspicion.[2] Let me briefly recapitulate that argument here, noting that much of what I wrote then has been extensively documented by David Naugle in his excellent study of worldview.

(1) It is striking that the term *Weltanschauung* was coined and popularized in the context of German Idealism and Romanticism, during that great flowering of the modern spirit that has dominated subsequent in-

---

2   A. Wolters, "On the Idea of Worldview and Its Relation to Philosophy," in *Stained Glass: Worldviews and Social Science,* edited by Paul Marshall, Sander Griffioen, and Richard Mouw (Lanham: University Press of America, 1989), 14–25.

tellectual history. The rapid spread of the concept and its cognates seems to be part of the pervasive influence of precisely that phase of German thought.

(2) A basic feature of that seminal period was the "rise of historical consciousness," a new awareness of the value of the historically singular. In reaction against the Enlightenment—indeed, against the whole millennial tradition of Greek intellectualism—a great reversal of values occurred wherein the universal was depreciated in favor of the particular, the abstract in favor of the concrete, the eternal in favor of the temporal, the identical in favor of the unique. Whereas previously the Western intellectual tradition had been oriented to the enduring "essence" or "substance" (*ousia*) of things, it now became oriented to the historical development (*Geschichtlichkeit*) of things.

(3) Generally speaking, we can say that the Greek word *philosophia* belongs to the thought-world dominated by *ousia* and that the German word *Weltanschauung* belongs to the thought-world dominated by *Geschichtlichkeit*. The two terms do have some features in common: *philosophia* and *Weltanschauung* both share a cognitive orientation to the whole, and both are associated with the optic metaphor of *viewing* (Greek *theōrein*, German *anschauen*). Where they differ is that the former places emphasis on the universal, abstract, eternal, and identical character of that viewing, whereas the latter places emphasis on the particular, concrete, temporal, and unique character of that viewing. Basic to the idea of *Weltanschauung* is that it represents a point of view on the world, a perspective on things, a way of looking at the cosmos from a particular vantage point that cannot transcend its own historicity. A worldview tends to carry the connotation, therefore, of being personal, dated, and private. This is not universally the case (notably in Engels' usage), but does seem to be at the root of the powerful attraction the idea of *Weltanschauung* has had for the modern West. A worldview may be more than individual—it may be collective (that is, held by everyone belonging to a given nation or class or period)—but, even so, it does not escape particularity, for it cannot transcend the experiences and perspectives of that particular nation, class, or period. Thus, worldview forfeits all claim to universal validity and becomes enmeshed in the problems of historical relativism.

(4) Whereas *philosophia* is highly theoretical and, therefore, reserved for an intellectual elite, *Weltanschauung* is broadly pretheoretical and, therefore, available to the mass of people. Furthermore, because philosophy is associated with science, worldview is considered to be nonscientific—which can be interpreted positively as *pre*scientific or negatively as *un*scientific.

(5) It is striking that the two primary features of *Weltanschauung* that we have highlighted, namely, that of being historically individual (private) and of being nonscientific (for the masses), also characterize the modern conception of *religion*. It is not surprising, therefore, that worldview has often been associated with religious faith, understood in the sense of a highly personal and pretheoretical commitment.

My conclusion is, therefore, that the notion of worldview has intimate historical and systematic connections with modern humanistic views of history, science, and religion. It is, in fact, virtually defined by those views. As I wrote in 1989, this leaves us with a crucial question: can Christians who are fundamentally critical of the spirit of modernity, particularly as it manifests itself in historicism, the autonomy of science, and the privatization of religion, salvage the idea of *Weltanschauung* for their own purposes?

To these objections to the Christian use of the category *worldview* we can add two others: the metaphor of "viewing" the world is both too intellectualistic, since it focuses on thought to the exclusion of action, and too oriented to seeing to the exclusion of the more biblical metaphor of *hearing*.

In my opinion, it is relatively easy to answer these latter two objections. The first one, that worldview is too intellectualistic to serve as a Christian category, rests on a double misunderstanding. In the first place, it assumes that those who advocate the concept of a Christian worldview are claiming that Christianity is a worldview and nothing else. This is patently false. Christianity is, first of all, the person of Christ and the Kingdom that he ushers in, and it includes the covenantal relation of Christ and the Church and everything involved in that. The imperfect cognitive "view" that people may form of reality in the light of the person and work of Christ is an important but subordinate part of Christianity as a whole, which can hardly compare with the forgiveness of sins and the life of sanctification. In fact, it is probably fair to say that a Christian worldview is only one part of an aspect, namely the cognitive aspect, of the life of sanctification. Secondly, the kind of cognition that is involved in a worldview is not primarily *intellectual* cognition. There is a lot more to knowing than scientific or theoretical insight, and worldview, in my opinion, is much more prescientific and pretheoretical than anything else.

The second objection, that worldview privileges seeing, whereas the Bible privileges hearing, is, in my opinion, based on a discredited way of contrasting Greek and Hebrew thought, associated with the well-known book by Thorleif Boman, *Hebrew Thought Compared to Greek* (E.T. 1960). In any case, the contrast fails to recognize that we can know more about the world by seeing than by hearing and overlooks texts in the Bible like Job 42:5, arguably the climax of the book of Job, where the hero of the story finally exclaims, "My ears had heard of you, but now my eyes have seen you." Here, seeing is clearly privileged over hearing.

But the other considerations that have been urged against the Christian use of the category *worldview* are in my opinion much more weighty. In its origin and widespread usage, *Weltanschauung* seems to depend for its meaning on conceptions of history, science, and religion that Christians ought to reject. I do not dispute that the term has historically had these associations. However, I would offer two reasons why these considerations are not decisive for rejecting worldview as a Christian category.

The first is that there is already a century-old tradition of using worldview in a positive Christian sense. As Naugle demonstrates, through the work of James Orr and Abraham Kuyper, the word *worldview* has undergone the same kind of transformation as the Greek *logos* in the Prologue of John. There is now a well-established Christian tradition in which worldview does *not* suggest historical relativism or the privatization of religion. Both Orr and Kuyper oriented their idea of a Christian worldview to a divine revelation and a constant world order that transcends historical particularity. Furthermore, they exploited a feature of the idea of *Weltanschauung* that is particularly congenial to the Christian religion, the fact that it is not restricted to people of a certain kind of intelligence or training. It is precisely its *non*intellectualist nature that allows a Christian worldview to appeal to and be appropriated by a wide range of people.

In addition, especially through the work of Kuyper, the idea of worldview was made to do the very opposite of what its historical origins might lead one to expect: to counter the idea of religion as a private affair and to insist that Christianity was public truth. Kuyper did this by insisting that the Christian worldview (he actually spoke of the *Calvinistic* worldview or world-and-life view) stands arrayed against such secular competitors as liberalism and Marxism as a spiritual and cultural force of the same order as these. Christianity was not to be marginalized, but was to be allowed to play a role in the struggle for cultural hegemony in the public square, pitting itself as a culturally formative worldview against other culturally formative worldviews in the arena of world history. In my opinion, it was a bold stroke of genius on Kuyper's part when he adopted and adapted the newly popular notion of *Weltanschauung* in the nineteenth century to put Christian cultural aspirations on a par with the ideological move-ments of the revolutionary age. It was through the notion of worldview that Kuyper gave Christianity renewed historical traction at a time when it was being dismissed as harmless private piety or the irrelevant academic discipline of theology.

But my second reason for not rejecting worldview as a valid Chris-tian category is the lack of a viable alternative. If we believe that Chris-tianity teaches the truth about reality and human life, and if we want to communicate to the world around us that this truth is public truth, with implications for the way human society and civilization ought to be or-ganized and shaped, what other word shall we give to our understanding of that truth? Shall we call it doctrine, or theology, or ideology, or system of values, or perspective? I would contend that a little reflection will show that each of these alternatives has drawbacks that are even weightier than those of "worldview." In the modern world, doctrine and theology sug-gest ecclesiastical and academic specialties that can safely be ignored in the real world, ideology still has overtones of class-related false conscious-ness, values suggests subjective and historically variable human valuation, and perspective is more reminiscent of relativism (think of perspectival-ism) than worldview ever was.

It is instructive to notice how many of the church fathers solved this problem in their day. As the French scholar Malingrey has docu-mented, they often chose the term *philosophia* to denote Christianity in its cognitive and world-claiming aspect.[3] This was a remarkable choice, since the only time the Scriptures speak of *philosophia* they speak of it as a pagan force to be warned against, representing the tradition of men as opposed to the tradition of Christ (Colossians 2:8). But these church fathers decided to claim the word for Christ and indeed spoke frequently of the *philosophia Christi*. We need to remember, of course, that in late antiquity, philosophy was as much a way of life (to which one was "con-verted") as an intellectual discipline and even as an intellectual pursuit included much more (mathematics, for example, and political science) than its modern namesake does. We still find echoes of this ancient usage in Erasmus and Calvin, but it has since died out or given the more specific meaning of a Christian approach to the contemporary academic discipline of philosophy. But in its early usage, it stands as a striking parallel to Orr and Kuyper's bold move in appropriating *Weltanschauung* for Christ.

My argument has been that there are decided disadvantages to using

---

3   Anne Marie Malingrey, Philosophia; *étude d'un groupe de mots dans la littéra-ture grecque, des Présocratiques au 4e siècle après J.-C.* (Paris: Klincksieck, 1961).

worldview in a positive Christian sense, but that on balance the advantages outweigh the disadvantages. We need to weigh the pros and cons and acknowledge that this weighing is a multifaceted thing on which Christians can easily disagree. Ultimately, I would contend, this is a matter of spiritual discernment applied to the strategic interests of Christian cultural engagement. But I acknowledge that to frame the issue in this way is to betray my own understanding of the overall relation between the spiritual and the cultural—in fact, it betrays what I would call my worldview, the world-and-life view that I was taught as a child in a Dutch neo-Calvinist home.

Concluding Unscientific Postscript

I borrow this phrase from Kierkegaard to describe some informal reflections that were sparked by previous speakers at the Cornerstone conference on worldview and that I added to my presentation of the above on the last day of the conference. There are three sets of additional comments that I would like to make.

(1) Perhaps there is a further difference between the heirs of Orr and Kuyper in the way they appropriated *Weltanschauung*. For Kuyper and the neo-Calvinists, the concept of worldview not only served to make Christianity a *competitor* of secular ideologies, but also served as the means through which faith was "operationalized," as it were, for the complexity of a differentiated society. Jim Olthuis is right that worldview is a *mediating* category, which helps to bring faith/the Gospel/Scripture to bear on matters not mentioned or addressed in Scripture, such as schools, labor unions, nation states, and modern technology. Worldview thus functions as a hermeneutical key for cultural engagement, both in the academy and beyond.

In the past, I have used the image of worldview as a *gearbox* that connects the power of the engine with the traction of the wheels. The animating drive of the Gospel as revealed in Scripture shapes and directs concrete activity ("where the rubber hits the road") through the mediation of a worldview. In the Reformational tradition, this mediation is further facilitated through a worked-out philosophical ontology, which, in turn, deals with the foundational issues of the various disciplines. This is a feature that is largely lacking in the tradition inspired by Orr.

This mediating function of worldview, whether or not it is accompanied by a refined systematic philosophy, is a key aspect of the way the term *Weltanschauung* has been "converted" for Christian use, at least in the Kuyperian tradition. Now admittedly, this makes for a certain *dis-*

tance between Scripture and the academic disciplines. In an overreaction to biblicism and naive proof-texting, it is certainly possible that a Reformational scholar will lose a direct and nurturing relationship with Scripture—to replace it, as it were, with a schematized understanding of worldview (e.g., creation-fall-redemption) or a particular systematic philosophy (e.g., a set of "transcendental ground ideas"). There is certainly a danger here.

The mediating function of worldview was already clearly laid out in the writings of Herman Bavinck. I refer here to my 1996 article on the relationship between faith and science in Bavinck.[4] In his view, aside from the theology, Scripture can be *directly* brought to bear on the academic disciplines only in history and then only in the ancient Near Eastern history to which the Bible itself testifies. Everywhere else, its normative bearing is mediated through a worldview, a worldview that is essentially constituted by biblical teaching on the origin, essence, and goal of things.

(2) Having said all of the above, I still feel a bit uneasy about the Christian use of worldview. I am reminded of Winston Churchill's quip about democracy: "Democracy is the worst form of government except for all those other forms that have been tried from time to time." There are many disadvantages to the term *worldview*, but are there any alternatives that have fewer disadvantages?

In casting about for such alternatives, I initially thought of the words *confession* (as in "confession of faith") or *mind* (as in "the mind of Christ" or the title of Harry Blamires' book *The Christian Mind*). But then, in light of Jim Olthuis's paper at this conference, I thought of the word *testimony*. Could we speak of the Christian *testimony* as the biblical alternative of the testimony of Marxism, or liberalism, or feminism? It strikes me that this term has a number of advantages:

   (a)   It is a central biblical concept.
   (b)   It does not privilege the visual or the intellectual.
   (c)   There is some historical precedent for this usage (see, for example, *The Contemporary Testimony* of the Christian Reformed Church).
   (d)   It highlights subjective involvement and experience.
   (e)   It is nevertheless oriented to truth as a given independent of the testifier.

---

4   A. Wolters, "Herman Bavinck on Faith and Science," in *Facets of Faith and Science,* edited by J. Van der Meer (Lanham: Pascal Centre–University Press of America, 1996), Vol. 4, 347–52.

(f)   It has an implicit reference to narrative.

(g)   It has the connotation of making an appeal to others.

(h)   It can be based on any of the five senses, but still privileges seeing, since generally the best witnesses are eyewitnesses.

In this connection, I am reminded of the opening sentences of the first epistle of John: "That which was from the beginning, which we have heard, which we have seen with our eyes, which we have looked at and our hands have touched—this we proclaim concerning the Word of Life. The life appeared; we have seen it and testify to it . . . ." Of course, this refers primarily to the early Christians' experience of Jesus Christ, not to the world in general, but it was an experience that transformed their perception of everything.

I throw this out as a possible alternative to the use of worldview. Can testimony do the same work that worldview does in mediating the Gospel for cultural engagement? Or is it too burdened by unfortunate connotations of its own in contemporary culture to communicate clearly? I leave it to others to judge.

(3) Finally, a word about worldview and spirituality. Among worldview enthusiasts, one can sometimes detect a somewhat dismissive attitude to such topics as spirituality and spiritual formation, meaning by those terms a focus on such traditional spiritual disciplines as prayer and meditation. This may be partly due to an awareness of the dangers of pietism, or a world-flight mentality, or a fear of emotionalism.

Although these cautions are fully justified, I wonder whether a tradition that spends much of its energy combating pietism is not in danger of losing a healthy respect for piety and the traditional "spiritual exercises" of the Christian tradition. My own journey in recent years has led me to explore the rich resources of Ignatian spirituality in an effort to compensate for this one-sidedness. In this connection, I am also reminded of a remark once made by my friend and colleague George Vandervelde (who incidentally was one of the authors of the CRC *Contemporary Testimony*) after he had read the manuscript of my book *Creation Regained*. He observed that it did not pay much attention to the practice of piety. In the twenty years since the book was published, I have come to recognize that this omission is indeed telling.

On the other hand, I must confess that I continue to be startled by the apparent inability of many devout Christians to connect their faith in anything but a moralistic way to the cultural and political issues of the day. For example, in my experience, there are many Christian students who are deeply committed to prayer evangelism (for example, in the charismatic movement), but who are woefully weak in relating their faith to their scholarship. They lack a worldview that can help them do that.

In my opinion, it is high time that the personal experience of God—in prayer, in tongue-speaking, in being "filled with the Spirit," and so on—be more fully integrated into the Christian appropriation of *Weltanschauung*. Perhaps I should say "reintegrated," since it was a mark of Abraham Kuyper, the great Dutch champion of the notion of a Christian worldview, that he had an intense devotional life. Perhaps there is something appropriately symbolic about the fact that I came to Grand Rapids, Michigan, in September 2004 to attend two gatherings. One was the academic conference on worldview at Cornerstone University, an institution rooted in the Baptist tradition. The other was the initial meeting of a synodical study committee on "Third Wave Pentecostalism" of the Christian Reformed Church, the chief conveyor of the Kuyperian emphasis on Christian worldview in North America. Perhaps there is a way in which the so-called "third wave" of the Pentecostal-charismatic movement and the neo-Calvinist tradition of worldview thinking can learn from each other. The fervent spirituality that characterizes the one and the worldview-mediated cultural engagement that characterizes the other are not, in my opinion, ultimately incompatible.

Response to Al Wolters on *Worldview*

James A. Herrick

Following his careful and convincing exploration of the history of the term *worldview*, Professor Wolters arrives at the conclusion that the term *worldview*, though not perfect, is the best we have at the moment. Despite the term's very real liabilities—especially for Christians—I believe that it remains a highly accessible and useful concept and that we should probably be reluctant to jettison it too quickly for some other term or concept.

There are a number of helpful insights and observations in Professor Wolters' paper, not only into the history of the word around which this conference is structured, but about the role of several prominent figures in the history of the modern struggle to keep Christianity relevant as a kind of public knowledge. I especially appreciated his observation that Abraham Kuyper "gave Christianity renewed historical traction at a time when it was being dismissed as harmless private piety or the irrelevant academic discipline of theology."

I think the point is also well taken that despite the term's deep roots in intellectual movements such as German Idealism, as Professor Wolters puts it, "it is precisely its *non*intellectualist nature that allows a Christian worldview to appeal to and be appropriated by a wide range of people."

My purpose here is to offer some musings and observations, prompted by Professor Wolters' paper, on the *pedagogical* uses of worldview. My defense of the term *worldview* as useful and even liberating focuses on the educational project rather than on history and etymology. I have, for about twenty years now, taught a course on worldviews—or so I have told my students. I teach the course every two or three years and have often used Jim Sire's highly accessible and wonderfully useful book *The Universe Next Door* as one of the texts. It introduces students to the basic categories and vocabulary of worldview—a contribution to their education not to be taken lightly, for having a vocabulary with which to talk about what one believes empowers and liberates. This is especially true in the current spiritual environment in which Christian students often are made to feel that their absolutism consigns them to the status of historical throwbacks or benighted ideologues. Moreover, the notion of worldview, freighted as it is with rational expectations, encourages and legitimates the project of examining and refining one's views.

A few years ago, a student in my course was reading a paper that presented an initial exploration of her worldview. Worldview was for her, as it is for many students, a new and intriguing idea. And, again as for many students, she was captivated by the very idea that she had a worldview that could be set out and discussed. She stated along the way in her paper that she believed in the Christian God. "And," she added—she said "and," not "but"—"and I believe in reincarnation." I asked her where her belief in reincarnation originated, and she said that her grandmother had believed in the concept, and she had learned more about it in a religion course at the college, and she had seen a program on TV on near-death experiences. "And where did your Christian beliefs originate?" I asked. My parents took me to church, she explained. Had she considered the possibility that the two ways of thinking—Christian and reincarnation-al—might be incompatible, I inquired. I hope that I ask such questions "gently and reverently," to borrow St. Peter's phrase, because such statements of belief are always deeply personal. "No," she replied, "I guess not."

In a different class just about two years ago, students were discussing whether religious people were "narrow-minded." One young woman in the class said, "It doesn't bother me what people say about religion. Last summer, I made up my own religion." I asked her about this, and she said that she had taken some ideas from Christianity and some from Buddhism and added some ideas of her own. I appreciated her candor, but was a little taken aback by the confidence with which she reported on her experiment in religious invention, experiments undertaken without any sense of a need for internal consistency or external coherence.

Then, just a few days ago in a class on popular culture, I showed the students the webpage of an organization called The Temple of Hip Hop. This new religion, which is how it presents itself, has a surprisingly well-developed set of spiritual doctrines, all of which draw in some way on the basic unifying principles of Hip Hop culture. I asked the students what they thought of this idea that two rap artists had just started a religion. One young man replied, "I do not see anything wrong with it. That's what people have done for hundreds of years. They say they are prophets, and they start religions." The students and I had just been talking about the singer Madonna's recent reinvention of herself as an advocate of ancient Jewish mysticism or Kabbalah, and her attendant name change to Esther. She has recently visited Israel on a fact-finding mission with much attendant media fanfare.

These brief narratives suggest, I believe, that the social world in which we and our students live and move and have our being is one of spiritual confusion and that the concept of worldview can be enormously helpful to students in finding their way through that confusion.

What Professor Wolters' paper prompted me to think about is just how powerful the concept of worldview has been in pedagogical circles over the past twenty years or so. Students whom I have worked with both here and in Eastern Europe have found worldview an illuminating and empowering idea. It is easy for faculty to forget that students today inhabit a phantasmagoric theatre of frenetic media images, raw emotion, and powerful appeals that undermine the self to make the sale. In most cases, their education and home life have provided them with precious few organizing moral concepts, let alone critical apparatuses for responding to this video arcade of the soul. The notion of worldview is, for many contemporary students, the doorway into genuine intellectual and even spiritual life, and it can and often does awaken in them some confidence in their own ability to reflect on, question, and, yes, organize their own beliefs.

But, just as important as its capacity to encourage rational examination and organization of belief and conviction, worldview, with its attendant sense of moral structuring of one's outlook on the world, grants students a life-saving capacity to respond sensibly to the commercially funded circus they encounter every day with its incessant in-your-face sexual posturing, its lures and lies, and its lunatic substituting of careless intimacy for love and shameless self-exposure for emotional authenticity. And then there is the terrifying helter-skelter of current geopolitics. To talk about worldview in the classroom in a morally authentic way that takes students' lived experience seriously can be to create an oasis in a desperate, bewildering desert.

The idea of worldview has been with us long enough that we are now wondering about how it can be improved and what comes next. But personal experience in the classroom tells me that the idea of a worldview is still new to many students both here and abroad. Worldview is a particularly exciting idea to young people who have never even been asked by any adult in any setting to think about what they believe and who want to talk and think carefully about this aspect of who they are. Talk of worldviews—precisely because of its capacity to engage matters such as belief, personal values, and one's moral orientation—prompts relevant and even exciting classroom conversations.

In sum, I appreciate both Professor Wolters' historical critique of the term as well as his affirmation that worldview can still be used with integrity by Christians. Though I have been convinced by things that I have heard at this conference that the concept is certainly worth revisiting, worldview has been and remains a remarkably useful construct for thousands of students. The opportunity to talk about their worldviews with people such as are gathered in this room has for many graduates of our faith-based institutions of higher education been perhaps the most powerful, informative, and life-shaping educational memory that they have taken away with them into what is often referred to as the real world.

Part IV
Worldview in the Classroom

Balancing the Antithesis: An Enduring Pedagogical Value of Worldview[1]

David V. Urban

In his September 2004 convocation speech, Calvin College president Gaylen J. Byker asserted that "[c]onducting and sustaining academic life *coram deo* . . . requires constantly embracing and balancing piety, common grace, and the antithesis."[2] As I pondered on President Byker's words in the days that followed, I was particularly intrigued by his challenge that we balance "engagement with God's world in recognition of the common grace that God grants to all of his creation" with "a constant awareness of and response to the antithesis"—defined by one source as "a recognition that there is an opposition between God's ways and the ways of a fallen world."[3] Keeping this balance in mind, I want to suggest that utilizing the rubric of worldview and incorporating basic worldview categories can be an effective way to teach the antithesis even as we keep common grace in full view. In doing so, we may honestly recognize and analyze substantive differences between Christianity and the philosophical bases of our subject matter while simultaneously recognizing and appreciating the genuinely redemptive aspects of such material. Such an approach can empower us to celebrate the common grace found in our subject matter even as we recognize the subject matter on its own ideological terms.

---

1   I would like to thank Calvin College for supporting the writing of this essay with a Calvin Research Fellowship. Thanks also to my colleague Jim Vanden Bosch, who read and commented on an earlier version of this essay, and to Roy Anker, who read and responded to the near-final version.
2   Gaylen J. Byker, *Academia Coram Deo* (Calvin College Convocation, Grand Rapids, MI, 7 September 2004).
3   John Netland and Loren Haarsma, eds., *DCM Reader: Calvin College* (Littleton, MA: Tapestry, 2005), 212.

I suggest, simply, that teachers be conversant with basic worldview categories and their characteristics and that we appropriately utilize these categories in our discussion of material that exhibits the characteristics of these worldviews, discussing such matters with our students so that they may better understand the ideological foundations for such material and the resultant presuppositions that accompany the material. By interacting with the worldviews exhibited by our subject matter in such a way, we may teach the antithesis in a way that does not merely point out the tension or conflict between views represented in our subject matter and those represented by Christianity; we may seek to better understand the worldview perspectives that these works embody. In my own experience, I have found the worldview categories set up by James W. Sire in *The Universe Next Door*—Christian theism, deism, naturalism, nihilism, existentialism, Eastern pantheistic monism, New Age, and postmodernism—to be extremely helpful for discussing the antithesis in this manner.[4] For those of us teaching in the Kuyperian tradition, my suggestion that we use a worldview-informed approach to teach the antithesis is, of course, nothing new. Kuyper himself does much the same thing in his 1904 essay "Common Grace and Science," in which he celebrates scientific progress made by secularists even as he points out and critiques their naturalistic empiricist assumptions.[5] But because I notice a tendency, at least in certain Reformed academic circles, to emphasize common grace to the point of minimizing or even dismissing the import of teaching the antithesis,[6]

---

4   James W. Sire, *The Universe Next Door: A Basic Worldview Catalog*, 4th ed. (Downers Grove: InterVarsity, 2004).
5   Abraham Kuyper, "Common Grace in Science," in *Abraham Kuyper: A Centennial Reader*, James D. Bratt, ed. (Grand Rapids: Eerdmans, 1998), 441–60.
6   Informal discussion with colleagues at Calvin College has supported my sense that pedagogical attention to the antithesis has waned in certain Reformed arenas. In addition, I witnessed particularly strong resistance toward teaching the antithesis during the concluding major event at Cornerstone University's "After Worldview: Christian Higher Education in Postmodern Worlds" conference, a panel discussion among the conference's five keynote speakers. During this discussion, which was immediately preceded by my own brief address to the conference, Calvin Seerveld of the Institute of Christian Studies directly took issue with my just-articulated suggestion that we use worldviews to teach the antithesis. He commented that he did not think we ought to teach the antithesis, and he then characterized teaching the antithesis as an instructor saying to different hypothetical viewpoints, "you're wrong, and you're wrong, and you're wrong" (18 September 2004, Grand Rapids, MI.). While I recognize a degree of hyperbole in Prof. Seerveld's words, I relay this incident to demonstrate both

I think it appropriate for us to revisit this matter intentionally.

Before discussing my own pedagogical adventures, I will interact briefly with the scholarship of two Calvin College colleagues, studies that emphasize conscientious Christian interaction with the culture and appreciation for the common grace found therein. As I do this, I will suggest that an appropriate incorporation of worldview-informed pedagogy could aid our instructional use of these studies, helping us balance the related emphases of common grace and antithesis. The first work (one that is required reading for freshmen at Calvin College), William D. Romanowski's *Eyes Wide Open: Looking for God in Popular Culture*, calls Christians to engage—boldly but with discernment—popular media. Although Romanowski's book, as its subtitle suggests, pays considerable attention to the common grace to be found in such media, Romanowski also encourages his audience to be aware of the antithesis (although he never uses the term itself) in these same media. Throughout his "Matrix for Analysis of Popular Artworks," he consistently asks his readers to evaluate the degree to which a particular artwork's portrayal of the various categories he outlines is consistent with a Christian perspective.[7] He also asks readers to consider what perspective this artwork's creator is "coming from,"[8] and this is precisely where an intentional engagement with matters of worldview could complement Romanowski's approach. For we and our students will be much more adept at identifying artists' perspectives and interacting with how they compare to a Christian perspective if we can recognize the worldviews these artists' works demonstrate. Our analysis can then more adeptly consider not simply *how* an artistic work is or is not consistent with a Christian perspective but *why*—and our students may increasingly become cultural discerners who recognize concrete manifestations of different worldviews, discerners who understand the philosophical bases for the art they consume and for the antithesis that art exhibits.

The second study is Roy M. Anker's *Catching Light: Looking for God in the Movies*. In his introduction, Anker makes clear his strong emphasis

---

an acute resistance to the teaching of the antithesis by a respected worldview scholar in the Reformed tradition and to note how, I hope, an appropriate use of worldview to teach the antithesis differs significantly from an unfortunate approach—perhaps one that Prof. Seerveld and others have witnessed—that simply dismisses perspectives that conflict with instructors' Christian positions.

7   William D. Romanowski, *Eyes Wide Open: Looking for God in Popular Culture* (Grand Rapids: Brazos, 2001), 156–61.

8   Romanowski, *Eyes Wide Open*, 145.

on common grace in cinema, asserting that "movies often seem to see the world as only the omniscient God sees it."[9] Anker's book offers much valuable insight into how careful viewers can recognize God's common grace at work in various movies' depictions of human suffering and longing and the hope for redemption, but I believe that he also retreats from worldview analysis where it could helpfully supplement his main thesis. I note specifically his eighth chapter, "Tracking the Force: Meaning and Morality in the *Star Wars* saga." In his analysis of the saga, Anker emphasizes Christian themes, affirming that it "culminates in a resplendent vision of servanthood, reconciliation, and a winsome portrayal of the new creation that awaits the cosmos" (221). Throughout the chapter, he notes various biblical analogies: Obi-Wan Kenobi rescues Luke "in Good Samaritan style" (222), and Kenobi's teaching about the Force— "It surrounds us, it penetrates us, it binds us all together"—"sounds strikingly similar to St. Paul's language in Ephesians 4:6, which invokes 'one God and Father of all, who is over all and through all and in all'" (224); Anker asserts that Luke becomes "something of a Christ figure" (225), and he points out Luke's "kenotic self-denial" in his choice to die for his father Darth Vader, an act Anker calls "a perfect rendition of the notion of substitutionary atonement" (235); Yoda, in teaching Luke, "echoes the prophecies of Isaiah about the coming Messiah" and "echoes Jesus' repeated counsel for spiritual purity in all aspects of life" (230); Darth Vader is "redeemed" through his own self-sacrifice for Luke, and "father and son meet in reconciliation and true communion" (236); finally, the conglomeration of reconciled characters at the conclusion of *The Return of the Jedi* "looks a lot like what the New Testament envisions as the constituency of the family of God" (238).

I have profited from Anker's analysis of the saga as a redemptive Christian parable, but I am also concerned by a statement in the chapter's final paragraph: "Some conservative religious people have fretted extensively about supposed 'New Age' influences" (242). Besides a brief mention of Judaism, this dismissive statement is the chapter's only specific reference to a worldview other than Christianity, although Anker does acknowledge that "Lucas takes elements from other world religions" (241). But for those conversant with Sire's worldview analyses (or something comparable to them), the Eastern pantheistic monist and New Age bases of Lucas's portrayal of the Force is quite recognizable, and one need

---

9   Roy M. Anker, *Catching Light: Looking for God in the Movies* (Grand Rapids: Eerdmans, 2004), 4. Quotes marked parenthetically in this and the following paragraph.

not be a hand-wringer or decry Lucas's saga to call attention to such matters. Most important, Kenobi's aforementioned teaching on the Force—which Anker connects to Ephesians 4:6 and the personal, monotheistic Christian God—sounds very similar to the Hindu notion of Brahman, "the essence, the Soul of the whole cosmos," "the one, infinite-impersonal, ultimate reality"[10]—and the impersonal *it* used to describe the Force throughout the saga is significant. In addition, as Sire points out, Yoda's aphorisms strongly exhibit "New Age metaphysics."[11] In mentioning these points, I do not suggest that Anker or anyone else change his or her redemptive emphasis. But I do advocate that we take opportunities to educate our students about the characteristics of various worldviews and to point out manifestations of these worldviews in the material we teach. In doing so, we may not only recognize common grace in such material, but also recognize systems of thought that are, to whatever degree, antithetical to a Christian perspective.[12]

I will now discuss two courses in which I have incorporated worldview-informed pedagogy. Worldviews appear most prominently in my first-year composition course, in which I use Sire's book as the central text.[13] Students are assigned the book in its entirety, with accompanying readings for the worldviews represented. For example, the chapter on deism is accompanied by short pieces by Voltaire and Benjamin Franklin, the chapter on naturalism is accompanied by Bertrand Russell's "Why I Am Not a Christian," and the chapter on existentialism is accompanied by an excerpt from Sartre's *Existentialism*. While not all assignments are explicitly related to matters of worldviews, several assignments require students to interact with these matters directly. One assignment asks students to write, in dialogue form, a conversation between a Christian theist, a deist, and a naturalist (students create their own characters) in which these individuals discuss their views on a number of theological issues as well as on a social issue of the student's choice. As this assignment

---

10 Sire, *The Universe Next Door*, 144. See page 174 for his explicit connection between the Force and "the Hindu Brahman."

11 Sire, *The Universe Next Door*, 145.

12 After reading an essentially final version of this essay, Anker made clear in a personal note that "when I teach *Star Wars*, I bring up the question of worldview in the context of evangelical criticism of the saga, urging students to factor that in as they derive their own readings of Lucas's work" (29 June 2005).

13 For discussion, from various perspectives, of the larger matter of religious issues in composition courses, see Elizabeth Vander Lei and bonnie lenore kyburz, eds., *Negotiating Religious Faith in the Composition Classroom* (Portsmouth, NH: Heinemann, 2005).

requires judicious incorporation of Sire's book into the dialogue, it trains students to work with critical material in their writing, a rhetorical exercise that helps prepare them for a broader use of sources in their upcoming research papers. More pertinent to the concerns of my present essay, this assignment challenges them to think from the perspective of worldviews other than their own; moreover, a short follow-up reflective essay challenges them to consider their own attitudes toward people who hold such views and to consider how their own presuppositions affect such attitudes. Regarding whatever social issue students choose to discuss, I emphasize that there is probably not a single "Christian/deist/naturalist" position on that issue, but that it is necessary for them to articulate a position in a way that is somehow consistent with the worldview of the given speaker.

Another assignment has students examine elements of and/or representations of one or more worldviews in a movie, of their choice, that would lend itself to such analysis. (I remind students here that most contemporary movies, like most people, do not consistently display a particular worldview throughout but are influenced by and/or portray various ones.) Memorable papers have discussed Eastern pantheistic monism in *The Lion King* and *Star Wars* (one paper on *Star Wars* emphasized specifically its relation to Taoism); how characters overcome nihilism in *Reality Bites* and *Chicken Run*; existentialism in *Free Willy* and *I Heart Huckabees*; postmodern elements in *American Beauty* and *Castaway*; and the conflict between Christianity and postmodernism in *Saved!* My course's research paper does not require students to explicitly address worldview concerns, but a number of students opt to do so. Their projects have included analyses of the ethics of cloning and stem-cell research; analyses of naturalism in Thomas Hardy's *Tess of the D'Ubervilles,* of nihilism in Kafka's "The Metamorphosis," of existentialism in Sartre's *No Exit*, of the tension between Mama's Christianity and Beneatha's naturalism in Hansberry's *A Raisin in the Sun*; and analyses of the New Age basis for therapeutic touch in nursing. Various other papers address worldview concerns in less explicit ways, and students are asked, in a follow-up reflection paper, to consider how their own worldview shaped their essay and was shaped by their essay.

I also incorporate worldview considerations into two shorter assignments. In one, students reflect on which worldview among nihilism, existentialism, and Eastern pantheistic monism they find most attractive (most opt for either the purposefulness of existentialism or the tranquility of EPM, although one underachieving student admitted a strong liking for nihilism); in another, students discuss a particular encounter they have had with some manifestation of either New Age or postmodernism (these have included playing New Age-influenced video games, witnessing the seduction of a brother by postmodern cigarette advertising, and participating in various conversations with friends and family that reveal postmodern attitudes). Amidst these different writing assignments and class discussions, students gain not only a greater understanding of how different worldviews influence the world around them, they recognize these worldviews at work in themselves and are challenged to reevaluate their lives in light of such recognition. During our discussion on deism, one student, perceiving her tendency to live as though God were not actively involved in the world, commented, "I say I'm a Christian, but I live like a deist." She expressed a desire, among other things, to pursue a more intentional prayer life. Another student wrote that she saw that her beliefs concerning abortion and homosexuality were strongly influenced by a postmodern mindset. Although she noted the inconsistency between these views and her Christianity, she also wrote that she had no plans to change her opinions on these controversial issues. Although these students' responses to their respective realizations differed significantly, both cases display how an application of worldview analysis to oneself can elicit recognition of an antithesis within one's own attitudes and actions.

I have also used worldview-informed pedagogy to teach the antithesis in my Modern Drama course. Although I do not assign Sire's text for this course (although I have recommended it to students in the course), I do make significant use of the concepts he outlines. Indeed, the worldviews that manifest themselves in particular plays do much to explain characters' actions, including actions that readers find particularly at odds with Christian ideals. The recurring line, "What else could I do?" (and its variations), that rings throughout Ibsen's *A Doll House* implicitly articulates the naturalistic assumption that people's situations and choices are determined by social structures; similarly, the title character's seduction at the hands of her valet Jean in Strindberg's *Miss Julie* is portrayed as the inevitable result of her upbringing and the physiological makeup she inherits from her mother; as noted before, the conflict between Mama and Beneatha in *A Raisin in the Sun* is largely based on their respective Christian and naturalistic worldviews; the hopelessly illogical universe of Beckett's *Endgame* is plainly nihilistic: belief in God is mocked as ridiculous, and Clov's attempt to create order himself, a clear satire of existentialism, is a comic failure; Jessie's resolution to kill herself in Marsha Norman's *'night Mother* can be seen as the existential decision of a woman who, having spent her life being controlled by family members and epilepsy, finally determines—once and for all—to control her own fate; in Hwang's *M. Butterfly*, Gallimard's enduring and, ultimately, willfully self-deluded belief that the cross-dressing spy Song Liling is actually his faithful female lover demonstrates a postmodern penchant for creating a reality that works for oneself apart from concerns of epistemological certainty.[14]

Discussion of worldviews in these plays also gives opportunities to identify redemptive elements amidst disturbing character actions. For example, although most Christians are uneasy with Nora's decision to leave her family at the end of *A Doll House*, we can still recognize that she is choosing to openly rise above her circumstances rather than merely be controlled by them; a similar assertion can be made about Jessie's suicide in *'night Mother*. While giving approval to neither divorce bereft of biblical mandate nor suicide, we may recognize the common grace of thoughtfully exercised free will in these actions, decisions that assert each individual's bearing the image of God, even as the decisions themselves arguably do more violence to that image than to remain in a thoroughly unredeemed situation. The tension between common grace and the antithesis is present here on a number of levels and can be the source of fruitful class discussion.

Before I conclude, I share a few points of caution I seek to heed when using worldviews in the classroom. First, I try to resist pigeonholing, and I encourage my students to do the same. Although some people, artworks, and so on consistently demonstrate a single, clearly identifiable worldview, many others will demonstrate an amalgamation of several worldviews, and it is more valuable to recognize elements of various perspectives than to try to fit every aspect of a particular book, movie, and so on into a particular worldview. Second, I try to be sensitive to the degree of "worldview training" students have already had. At my previous institution, a Baptist college in the Southwest where my composition students were almost exclusively first-semester freshmen, most of whom had been educated at public schools, students demonstrated great eagerness to learn worldview categories and apply them to their writing, and their enthusiasm resulted in intellectually stimulating essays that displayed incisive worldview-informed analysis. The four fall-semester courses of freshman composition I taught there, based on students' written work and evaluations, were resoundingly successful. I

---

14   These plays can be found in Lee A. Jacobus, ed., *The Bedford Introduction to Drama*, 4th ed. (Boston: Bedford, 2001).

received a similar response from my first fall-semester composition class at Calvin College, even though most students there attended Christian high schools. The response from my spring-semester composition students (at Calvin, roughly half of the first-year students take composition during the fall and half during the spring) was not nearly so positive. While a number of factors contributed to this, one factor was a kind of "worldview overload"; the matter of worldview had been discussed in a number of forums already at Calvin (as well as in high school for some), and I met resistance from the onset. The next time I taught composition during the spring, I intentionally omitted material that would overlap with previous courses, and I consciously avoided potentially off-putting terminology. (For example, I found myself substituting the word *perspective* for *worldview* many times.) Finally, I try not to let worldview concerns intrude where they should not. In teaching modern drama or other literature, I include worldview discussion only as appropriate to better understand the literature itself. In my composition class, I am increasingly vigilant not to let worldview concerns detract from sufficient focus on the mechanics of writing.

These caveats aside, I remain a strong believer in worldview-informed pedagogy. As this present volume illustrates, the overall concept of and use of worldview has developed in various ways and continues to evolve. It is a wheel that is being continually oiled and retuned (and perhaps even reinvented, for better or for worse), and there is disagreement aplenty regarding how to apply it. But whatever we do, let us not throw the wheel away. In the classroom and elsewhere, it remains a valuable tool with which to negotiate the tension between common grace and the antithesis. And by all means, let us keep teaching our students how to recognize common grace; at the same time, let us not think that common grace abounds in their lives to so great an extent that they do not need some intervention on our part to recognize the antithesis.

Response to David V. Urban

ROY M. ANKER

I appreciate very much Professor Urban's very gentle effort to flag the deterioration of my antithetical impulses. He is, in fact, so scrupulous and gentle that I wonder if the critique is a very good example of the tendency to mush antithesis analysis. In response, I will raise questions not so much about Urban's reading but of the limiting tendencies of the antithetical impulse with specific reference to evangelical criticism of the *Star Wars* saga.

First, antithesis perspectives tend not to work well with literature, an art form that thrives on the dramatization of ambiguity, life amid the "middle" that is the human condition, as John Updike points out with special indebtedness to Karl Barth, himself an emphatic devotee of the antithesis. The whole point is that life rarely fits neatly into taxonomies of human contrivance (and it assumes a kind of ahistorical purity in the tradition of Christian thought). Antithesis thought is especially challenged when confronting fable or parable, for the method of both, and the foundation for their effectiveness is to cloak metaphysical truth till the unexpected narrative turn that provides the story's final resounding wallop of revelation. The form demands the unsettling experience of murk and ambiguity. In contrast, the antithetical impulse is far more comfortable with clear, tidy demarcations that separate the sheep from the goats—or the Hindus from the Christians. It seeks reassurance rather than wrestling and clarity.

As for the fretfulness of antithesists, the habit of critics of *Star Wars*, the venerable James Sire included, is to point to a single, and usually very incidental, line that in some measure seems theologically problematic (admittedly, Urban is careful not to do this, though he has Sire do it for him). Its presence in the story then gives ample warrant to dismiss the whole of the venture, thus vacating the intentions and means of whole literary imaginative enterprise. Very often, the problematic line supersedes and subverts all that the narrative itself illumines, and it is to ask the form to be something other than what it is, namely theology instead of a fantastical mode of storytelling.

Second, interpretation is an amply demanding business, and movies generally set out to ring as many of the viewers' chimes as possible by any and every means possible. Where one hears St. Paul, another hears the Buddha. That discounts the fact that, at times, Paul (or John) sounds very unlike Paul and rather New Agey, as Paul does in that Ephesians passage. In these instances of problematic resonance, it is best to defer to the shape of the story itself—to put, in other words, the words in context of the tale. In the story Lucas tells, the narrative and the language lie a whole lot closer to Christian theology than to Asian theologies. Yanking lines out of context is, in general, not a very good way to talk about anything.

Last, antithesist folks seem inconsistent, extending tolerance to those they know are fellow travelers that they do not extend to those whose religious commitments they do not know. So it is that C. S. Lewis and J. R. R. Tolkein are much praised, even though their works contain notions that are far more problematic than anything that Lucas ever sets forth. For example, in *The Lion, the Witch, and the Wardrobe*, Lewis stocks his story with all manner of mythology and the occult—fauns, satyrs, magic, and even white witches—and he never gets anywhere close to overtness about his Christian belief; one could even argue, and persuasively, I think, that Lucas goes much further in spelling out the nature of the Christian God than does Lewis (this is the nine-hundred-pound gorilla with which the makers of the new live-action Hollywood version of *The Lion, the Witch, and the Wardrobe* are now wrestling).

Contributors

Roy M. Anker is Professor of English at Calvin College, Grand Rapids, Michigan.

J. Matthew Bonzo is Associate Professor of Philosophy at Cornerstone University, Grand Rapids, Michigan.

James A. Herrick is The Guy VanderJagt Professor of Communication at Hope College, Holland, Michigan.

Craig Mattson is Associate Professor of Communication at Trinity Christian College, Palos Heights, Illinois.

David Naugle is Professor of Philosophy at Dallas Baptist University, Dallas, Texas.

James H. Olthuis is Senior Member emeritus in Philosophical Theology, Institute for Christian Studies, Toronto, Ontario.

George N. Pierson is Associate Professor of Philosophy, Trinity Christian College, Palos Heights, Illinois.

Aron Reppmann is Associate Professor of Philosophy, Trinity Christian College, Palos Heights, Illinois.

Calvin Seerveld is Senior Member emeritus in Philosophical Aesthetics, Institute for Christian Studies, Toronto, Ontario.

Michael Stevens is Associate Professor of English, Cornerstone University, Grand Rapids, Michigan.

David V. Urban is Assistant Professor of English at Calvin College, Grand Rapids, Michigan.

Albert Wolters is Professor Emeritus of Religion, Theology, and Classical Studies at Redeemer University College, Ancaster, Ontario.

CPSIA information can be obtained
at www.ICGtesting.com
Printed in the USA
BVHW09s2148111018
529907BV00002B/560/P